Get Up
and
Do It!

By the same authors:

The Effective Way to Stop Drinking (Beechy Colclough)
It's Not What You Eat It's Why You Eat It (Beechy Colclough)
A Challenge to Change (Beechy and Josephine Colclough)

Get Up and Do It!

ESSENTIAL STEPS TO ACHIEVE YOUR GOALS

BEECHY AND JOSEPHINE COLCLOUGH

ACTIVE

BBC Active, an imprint of Educational Publishers LLP, part of the
Pearson Education Group
Edinburgh Gate
Harlow
Essex CM20 2JE
England

First published 2004
Reprinted 2007

ISBN: 978-0-563-48765-4

Commissioning Editor: Emma Shackleton
Project Editor: Mari Roberts
Copy-editor: Kate Quarry
Designed by: Ann Thompson
Production Controller: Neil Wilmot

Printed by Hobbs

The Publisher's policy is to use paper manufactured from
sustainable forests.

*To all those who have shared their
lives and work with us*

Contents

Introduction

Get Up and Do It! is a motivational workbook that will give you the tools, strategies and insight to achieve your goals.

First, we'll talk about the processes that come into play when anyone considers doing something that will create a change, large or small, in their life. Human beings are rather curious creatures when it comes to coping and dealing with change. Change, whether 'good' or 'bad', can be stressful, and our natural reactions are often fear, anxiety or resistance – one of the big reasons why we sometimes think about change and then do nothing. It's part of being human, and the trick is to turn this fear or hesitancy into a positive.

We believe that people need to understand more about themselves in order to foresee blocks and self-sabotage and deal with them effectively. Some people are so afraid of failure they don't even try because then, they reason, they don't have to face things going wrong. They've already written the failure script. This book will put you into a 'can do' frame of mind so that you can stop sabotaging yourself and start to do things differently.

We also believe that the roots of success lie in preparation. This book helps you to do your groundwork, so that your journey to your goal does not get derailed by the unexpected. One of the tools for achieving this, for example, is an exercise in which you teach someone to be you for a day. To do this, you write down a typical day from start to finish, recording thoughts and feelings as well as events. This is highly revealing once you've thrown yourself into it.

We also ask you to do a general inventory about yourself – your skills, your assets, and areas that you can improve upon. For this we suggest the 'gremlin exercise'. It's not as mad as it sounds. The gremlin exercise is about you project-ing all the doubts you feel into a character called your gremlin, who is the source of your negative internal dialogue. This is a 'fun' exercise on the surface, but has an incredible punch to it. You could start to get very cross with that gremlin who keeps holding you back.

Motivation is a huge key to success, so you need to work on that. The more you feel like a success, the more you will behave like a success, and the more you will be a success. You'll go far once you've started to work on telling yourself: 'I can do it', 'I deserve to do it', and 'I will do it'. We have different exercises throughout the book to help you build your confidence and motivation, and many of the strategies are multi-dimensional: not only do they help you to plan and stay on track but they also help keep you motivated.

Something else we encourage you to do is keep a diary, so that you can take some time at the end of each day just to check where you are. You will see, as you work through the book, that we suggest you do quite a lot of lists too. *This is your workbook, so we've left space for you to write things down here and now as soon as they come to you.* And writing is an important part of making your goal happen, because you sit down and think, and commit yourself to paper.

We also encourage you to have a little 'coach' on your shoulder – just like a football or tennis coach – who will help you stay on track and shout encouragement to you. We call this your 'positive self-talk'.

We urge you not to misunderstand or misjudge the processes involved and the forces that come into play when you set about trying to achieve your goal. You might say, 'But all I want to do is stop smoking,' and, yes, quite right, that is a simple goal. However, it's a powerful drug and a comforting habit. People are going to notice that you've stopped, so you might feel exposed. Suddenly a simple goal looks different, doesn't it? *That doesn't mean you can't do it.* It just means you really need to understand how you feel about setting your particular goal.

The journey towards your goal might not be a smooth one. You need to be prepared for setbacks, and not abandon the goal just because the going gets tough. Some people see a problem as a sign that the goal is not achievable. Successful people – and you can be among them – know that problems are important staging posts along the way. You can't abdicate responsibility by saying, 'It's bad luck – I'm just not lucky. Things never go right for me.' You have to take charge of your goal – it's yours and you have to drive it over rough ground on occasions, and not give up.

An important technique we show you is how to make your own personal 'video', which you can play in your head to keep you on track. You imagine and learn to feel the feelings that you will have when you achieve your goal, and you keep playing these scenes over and over again.

We also point out that you don't have to do everything perfectly – all you have to do is your best, and your best is good enough. Say, for example, your goal is to get fit – that means 'fit' in terms of your age, health, current level of fitness and weight. Don't set a target that is unrealistic, or a target that feels like second best – the important thing is that you feel good about what you are doing, and that you don't think your regime has to be like anybody else's.

The twenty-first century is an age of constant change: our lives are marked by uncertainty, whether in our careers, finances, relationships, family or personal circumstances. It is now up to us to harness that force in our lives and turn it to our benefit. It's time to look at all aspects of our lives with an open and questioning mind. It's time to set the goals and be in charge of the changes those goals will bring.

▶
▶
▶   We suggest you read the book from cover to cover the first time. There-
▶   after, you are sure to want to return to parts of the book from time to time
▶   in order to refresh yourself about your plans and perhaps re-boot your
     thinking. To help you do this, we've highlighted the key ideas that will give
     you a surge of new energy with this zig-zag bar.

We sincerely hope that you make good use of this book and that you let your dreams come true.

Enjoy your journey. May it be an interesting and rewarding one.

Give yourself a chance!

Chapter 1
Understanding

❏ Do the groundwork

❏ Deal with fear (False Evidence Appearing Real)

❏ Anxiety doesn't have to be a bad sign

❏ The CHANGE commandments

Before you begin to work on your goal you need to do some groundwork. It is crucial for you to understand the task ahead, the processes involved and the forces that can come into play when you try to achieve your target. No matter how much we want something to happen, we're still capable of tripping ourselves up along the way – unless we are well prepared.

What does it take to achieve a goal? It's not necessarily about willpower, aptitude or skills. It's more about self-image and the messages we send ourselves. If we can see the outcome of the change and believe ourselves deserving of it, we're much more likely to get there. People label themselves as those who do and those who don't, and negative beliefs pretty much determine a negative end result, but anyone can challenge and change their self-labelling. We are going to show you how.

You need to be willing to give yourself the best chance to achieve what you want. So, don't be half-hearted and don't sell yourself short. But if it were that easy, we'd be sending you the formula on a postcard instead of writing a book! It's a journey, and an enjoyable and rewarding one. Take the time to read through this chapter, think about your goal and understand that any one of us can sabotage ourselves, consciously or subconsciously. This sabotage can be very subtle – in fact, it can be so subtle that some of you will be reading this and already thinking of moving on to the next chapter. Please don't!

◼ Why we resist change

All human beings find change difficult at some level. The degree may vary, but our reactions are similar. Many of you who work in large organizations will have taken part in seminars and courses about 'change management'. If you haven't, we're sure that you will have been exposed to changes that result from reorganization, redundancies and so on. You can tap back into your reactions to these events and think about how you felt. There can be fear, resistance or anger, or feelings of powerlessness and loss of control. Even if you speak to people about change that involves something positive, such as a promotion or a house move, there will be similar feelings, and probably the only difference will be the anger that comes when a change is perceived as negative. Everyone will feel, for example, a degree of resistance. Life, however, is about change. Birth and death are the big ones! These are also among life's most stressful experiences:

Divorce
Marriage
Moving house
Changing job

Some of these could be considered positive events, but they are still stressful. Why? Because they involve change and so they involve making decisions that have a powerful impact upon the immediate, if not long-term, future. They involve choosing one thing over another and closing other options. So, change that comes from pursuing goals involves stress and fear. The fear can often come from thoughts such as: 'Supposing I make the wrong decision?' 'Supposing something better comes along?' 'Supposing I challenge something in my life and it closes off other options?' 'Supposing something bad happens if I express that I am not happy or want more?' Or the really big fears: 'Supposing I fail?' and 'Supposing I'm wrong?' Have you noticed how often the word fear appears in this paragraph. FEAR is an interesting acronym:

False
Evidence
Appearing
Real

Think about something that you are fearful of. We will use the example of failure because it is a very relevant fear. Let's hear from Jeremy who wants to learn to drive:

> I'm very embarrassed because I'm 30 and have never even sat in the driving seat of a car. I was brought up in a big city and I always found the traffic very intimidating. Well, I have decided to learn to drive because I want to change my job and not being able to drive will be a negative. When I think about driving I feel really fearful. I actually picture myself on the day of my test and how miserable I will feel and how my friends will laugh at me.

Notice how Jeremy has all of these negative pictures created by his fear. Not only does he have negative images of something that hasn't even happened, but because those pictures are so vivid he even has the feelings he would experience if that event was a reality. So the pictures (what he imagines when he is fearful) are the 'false evidence', as we call it. Those images are very powerful and create strong feelings, despite the fact that none of it has happened. None of it is a reality, yet look at the impact!

▧ All talk and no action

Think about a goal that you have recently had, or one that you can remember with some clarity. We were talking to Peter, who is in his thirties, about this:

> I have a goal of starting my own business. I have a very solid business plan, which has been put together through a lot of hard work and discussions with peers and friends who can give me some useful input. I find though that I am talking and have been talking about doing it for about a year now and I just haven't moved it forward. I found it did move along whilst I was doing the research and the practical discussions, but something has happened and I just feel stuck. Having done a lot of talking and some action I have ground to a standstill.

The more we talked to Peter the more it became apparent why Peter is holding himself back. He did brilliantly in carrying out the research and considering all the practical aspects – in fact, he was completely faultless at this. Some people would have found making such a detailed plan a major obstacle, so he should feel very positive about it. As we spoke to him and questioned him further, Peter opened up and became clearer about what was holding him back:

> Something that holds me back is the fear of failing. You can probably see that I am a practical and methodical person. I have done lots of preparation and 'done my sums', so to speak. The next stage feels to me as if I am putting my fate 'into the lap of the gods'. I suppose I feel that the next bit is out of my control and that scares me. I smile as I say that because that's a real key to my inertia – I like to feel in control and I tend to lead my life having things and doing things that feel in my control. Going after my goal means me doing something that I don't like – I don't feel comfortable with.

Here is an excellent illustration of a prime reason why people resist change and therefore get in the way of achieving goals. Moving towards the goal involves 'going out of control', or so it seems to Peter and many other people. For him and others getting out of control is something that creates fear, is a state that is avoided as much as possible in their everyday lives and therefore is something that rings an alarm bell. As a result, Peter's experience tells him (incorrectly) that being 'out of control' is always a negative, but it really doesn't have to be that way. Now that Peter understands this, he is resolved not to be held back by that fear, and the very fact that he can now understand what is happening to him actually makes him feel a bit more in control.

As you work your way through this book and start to formulate your goal you will need to be able to identify possible blocks to progress. We have devoted Chapter 4 to this because it is a major hurdle for everyone. Just to help you start to think about blocks, think about some goals that you have had recently and can remember specifically. If you did not succeed with your goal ask yourself:

1 How do you feel about taking risks?
2 Do you have examples in your life that tell you whether you approach risks positively or negatively?
3 Do you have an over-exaggerated need for control? Understand that we all need to feel in control, so this does not make you a control freak, but assess whether your need for control is too great.

Think about strategies that you use in other areas of your life. Are you, for example, quite scientific/objective?

Do you look for empirical evidence?
Do you look at statistics or probability?
Do you want some tangible evidence that something will succeed?

Being methodical like this can be very useful under many circumstances, but there will also be times when it can hold you back. A great example is choosing a life partner. A scientific strategy won't work here because you can't get hard evidence of a successful outcome; you can only judge from how things feel now and project that into the future. People we have worked with have often found it very difficult to make up their minds about such issues because there is no way of testing the concept other than by doing it. Anyone who comes up with a 100 per cent successful test to predict the outcome of a relationship will become a billionaire.

Or are you not at all methodical about moving towards a goal?

Stopping smoking is a useful illustration. Many people who want to stop smoking will not utilize strategies that involve looking at research, evidence and up-to-the-minute treatments that can help them. In this, as in other situations, finding concrete evidence can improve your chances of success. Later in the book we will help you think about maximizing your chances of success by doing some things differently.

■ Having a different conversation

One of the things that you will be very aware of is that inside your head it is never still and quiet. What we mean by that is that everyone is always thinking about something and always saying things to themselves. Some of those thoughts almost sound like an internal conversation. Imagine, for example, that you have recently given up smoking and someone offers you a cigarette. You say, 'No, thank you', but somewhere inside your head this voice starts up: 'Oh, I'd like one really – could I just have one? Would it really matter?' Someone else might be thinking about applying for a new job. They have sent off for an application form and are reading it feeling all excited when that voice starts up again: 'Don't bother, you won't get it' or 'Who do you think you are? That's a bit good for you, isn't it?'

Think of how you have talked to yourself about a goal that you have had in the past. Make sure that you have a specific example. If you don't think about specific examples you might not benefit from the exercises we ask you to do. To be specific you must think about an example that you clearly remember – instead of 'Oh yes, when I set goals I always ...' try to do this: 'Yes, I remember when I wanted to move. I spent several afternoons going around the areas I was interested in and visited the local lettings agents ...' We are sure that you can see the difference between speaking generally and speaking specifically. So whenever we ask you to think about your previous goals and think about what happened, make sure that you only refer to the specific.

Jane is a good example of someone who starts off all positive and then starts finding the negative. Jane is the world's expert on dieting. She has been on every diet possible for a very short time. She has good positive discussions with herself, makes a start and then the counter-arguments begin: 'This is going to be so tough,' 'I'll never keep this up,' 'Perhaps I'm one of nature's fat people,' 'I'm useless at sticking to anything.'

Why does Jane – or anyone – do this? Some of you will say that she is making excuses, which could be correct. Certainly there will be people who fail because they really don't want to make the effort, and it is important to acknowledge that achieving goals often requires a lot of effort. That effort, though, can be well worth investing. Most of Jane's statements are, firstly, about her perception of how difficult sticking to her goal will be and, secondly, that she is someone who can't stick to anything. We are sure that she has evidence to back this up, but we are also sure that if we challenged her by saying, 'You really can't stick to anything? You have never completed anything?' her honest answer would be that that was not true.

Let's put that to the test by asking Jane the direct question:

Have you never stuck to anything?
Jane: 'Well, no, that's not true, there are some things I see through.'
Why do you say that, given what you have just said?
Jane: 'It feels like I never stick to anything that gets really hard.'

That sounds very different, doesn't it?

Let's look at the perception of any goal being hard. The smoker who is giving up will be preoccupied with how many hours and minutes it has been since their last cigarette. The dieter will be obsessed by how little they have eaten and how few calories they have had. All of it will feel very difficult and stressful and there will be a feeling of deprivation, of having given up some-thing. There will also be a lot of concern about how long it can really last. There will be questions like, 'How much longer can I keep this up?', and a feel of a constant internal struggle as though you are battling against yourself, at war with your own willpower.

■ Positive self-talk – choosing your words carefully

It is almost impossible for you to feel motivated if you consider that you are depriving yourself or suffering. Telling yourself that you are suffering is the kind of 'talk' that will get you back into the situation you are trying to change. You need to watch out for that talk because it will talk you right back to where you started! You need to be talking to yourself about the positive. So, rather than counting the hours and minutes since your last cigarette in a negative way you need to learn to 'reframe' it and make it feel positive. This is the key to 'positive self-talk', and we will be discussing this more as we go through the book. Let's look at an example:

Lucy hasn't smoked for a week. We ask her how she's feeling and what she's been thinking: 'Well, it's been 168 hours roughly since I last smoked. I'm not really feeling very good. I'm feeling very tense, really wondering whether I can keep it up.'

We talk to Lucy for a while and ask her if she can say something positive or say the same thing more positively. She replies:

Actually, if I say I haven't smoked for a week that sounds better than the hours business because I just feel dramatic when I say how many hours it is since I last smoked. I can also tell myself that it is early days and that I'm pleased I've got this far. Also, I really want to do it and I'm afraid that I'll mess it up.

When you are working on your goal it is so important to keep telling yourself as many positive things as possible so, looking at the above, some positive self-talk would be:

'I'm pleased I've got this far.'
'I really want to do this.'
'Haven't I done well not smoking for a week!'

If, for example, you have stopped smoking, talk about what you are starting rather than what you have stopped. Keep your focus on the goal, not the difficulties you have to go through to get there. Rather than thinking about difficulties you need to think about your solutions and strategies. Understand that if you keep telling yourself that what you are doing is hard then you will, understandably, feel like giving up. You can end up talking yourself out of doing whatever it is you have set out to do. So, from now on you need to talk yourself into completing your goal rather than finding 'opt-out clauses'.

You will also do better if you have researched your goals, where necessary. There may be some hard facts that will help motivate you through difficult periods. Think about the goal of stopping smoking once more. Getting out of this habit becomes easier as time passes. For example, many reformed smokers say that the worst times are during the first seven to ten days. Bearing this in mind, there is a huge clue that on day five of not smoking one of the things that you need to say to yourself is that it truly will not always be this hard – in fact, you should congratulate yourself for completing the hardest bit. No one would stop if every day of the process was so challenging. So, sometimes this positive self-talk can actually be backed up by research, meaning you need to be informed about the goal that you are pursuing – there really are times when certain pieces of information can be key to keeping you motivated.

Break negative patterns

It isn't good enough to say, 'This is me and I can't change' – we're afraid we don't buy that. We believe that everyone can make changes and we strongly encourage people to break negative patterns. Negative self-talk or filling yourself with negative messages are patterns that can be changed. If you think about it logically, you have practised and reinforced your patterns for years, so it is going to take time to change them, but it can be done. Stop making yourself into a helpless victim of something that clearly doesn't work and start believing that you can change aspects of yourself that hold you back and are simply unhelpful and disabling. You need to start behaving as if it really is going to happen.

We are all creatures of habit to some extent, and it is important for us to understand how we comfort ourselves with patterns that we have created and followed. These perform two very important functions. First, they give you that important feeling of control and, second, the safety of familiarity. That is fine if the patterns work for you. When they don't, people tend to condemn themselves with messages like, 'Well, that's just me,' and, 'You can't teach an old dog new tricks.' That is just not true. As you move through your life it makes sense to believe that you will have to find new ways of dealing with situations that may arise and that your repertoire will, therefore, have to be widened accordingly. It may also be that later on in life you gain the confidence to let go of strategies and patterns that just don't work or haven't worked for a long time.

▓ Don't misread anxiety as a bad sign

We have already talked about how change is stressful regardless of whether you perceive the change to be positive or negative. Here is another way of looking at what happens:

> Imagine driving in thick snow. If other cars have gone before you there will be a track worn in the snow. If you stay in the groove made by others, your vehicle will be easier to handle and you just continue on your way. Well, your habits and patterns are a bit like that groove in the snow. Some things feel almost automatic, and when you respond as you always do, it will feel effortless. In fact, you may not even notice that you are doing it. So, to continue the analogy, if you decide that you are going to drive out of that groove, then some obvious thing will happen. The car will become difficult to handle. The journey becomes bumpy and your heart will be beating a little faster because you are anxious. You will have to concentrate much harder.

Get the idea? So don't be put off by the fact that changing evokes feelings that may be quite uncomfortable – that is natural. Don't always see unpleasant symptoms as a warning sign, as they are not – it's just that you are doing something differently. Most goals and the changes they can bring, or the changes you have to make to reach a goal, can generate anxiety. Let's take Steve, who is thinking about changing his job:

> I know that I'm not great about taking risks. I'm a methodical person who will think things through. I've been speaking to some agencies and looking

at advertisements and I'm pretty sure that I am being underpaid by about 25 per cent and there are also aspects of the organization I work in that I am not happy with. The agencies I have spoken to have given me job specifications that will use all of my skills and will pay me more, but each time I think of taking that next step to achieving my goal my stomach churns, I feel a bit breathless, my palms sweat. I just feel really anxious. I think that there must be something that is worrying me but I am just not facing it.

What Steve is doing is taking the anxiety as a sign that there is something wrong, or that he is making a bad decision. He is almost using his anxiety as a barometer: 'If I didn't feel this then I would be making the right decision.' What Steve needs to realize, and what anyone in a similar position needs to realize, is that feeling anxious about pursuing a goal is actually quite normal. It is not a sign of doing something wrong or stupid. As we said earlier, going through change is stressful because of the very nature of the experience. The stress can vary from mild to strong, depending upon the goal that you are pursuing, your personality and your circumstances.

■ Seeing your goal in context and understanding your circumstances

Goals cannot be ranked in terms of ease. A difficult goal for one person could be easy for another and vice versa. So although we will talk about other people's blueprints for success, you must always allow yourself to understand how your personal circumstances and your own self can impact upon you achieving a goal.

We also need to say that there will be times when not attaining a goal could be spelling out loudly and clearly that you may need some professional help. If something repeatedly does not work for you – like trying to diet or cut down on your drinking – do not try to ignore it. Some people's problems may go beyond what a book like this can help with. Don't hear this as a negative – we need to be realistic. This book is not about labelling people who have difficulties as 'failures', but it does say that there are some issues that cannot be helped by a book alone. You can learn from the experience that you have the willingness and honesty to confront a problem, and then go and look for someone to give you additional help.

There are also circumstances that make it extremely difficult for people to concentrate upon themselves. You may have young children or elderly parents to care for. Perhaps a member of your family is in poor health. You may be under a lot of pressure at work and have to work long hours. There are many circumstances that are not excuses: they are a hard reality that can make achieving a goal very difficult. In the planning chapters – 7 and 8 – we will get you to look at what is feasible and attainable.

Again, one of the things that we want you to do is be realistic in setting goals and time frameworks. Sometimes people fail because they expect too much of themselves and set too high a target, rather than being realistic and attempting to achieve a goal stage by stage, giving themselves adequate time to do what they need to do.

There will be others who just feel that they have to rush at any goal that they set without thinking about it or giving themselves the tools to make it work. It is often better to set a smaller goal, achieve it and then move on rather than setting one that feels too great from the outset. Weight loss is a good example of this. If you have 4 stones to lose do you need to make that your goal, or would you do better to set out to lose 5 lb and then set another target when you have achieved that?

A key issue in attaining goals is to remain motivated. Many people have a particular skill in de-motivating themselves without even trying! Achieving an interim goal will give you the strength, drive and motivation to set another one. Remember this:

Happiness comes when expectation meets outcome.

Having said that, we are not saying that there are circumstances when you shouldn't try to achieve your goal. If you have a goal in mind we would always encourage you to go for it because you, like any human being, need a sense of achievement and fulfilment. It may be that your circumstances make it very difficult for you to concentrate on yourself, but we are sure that if you really want to then you can make some time for yourself, even if it is only a very small amount. Don't let lack of time deter you. You are allowed to take as many months as you need to achieve your goal if, from day to day, time available to spend on yourself is in short supply.

To summarize some of these points try to remember as you work towards achieving your goal:

The six commandments of change

C Commitment to change

H Hard work

A Anchoring yourself

N No negatives – but be realistic

G Goals – be specific

E Easy does it

When it comes to thinking about, clarifying and beginning the steps towards achieving your goal, we have one final point to make: you should really try to enjoy the journey. There is a lovely expression that comes up a lot in personal development books: 'Don't just focus on the final destination, concentrate on the journey that you are making.' Be clear what your final destination is, think about the route that you want to take, and be realistic about how far you can travel in one go. Don't make the journey so long that you feel exhausted when contemplating the way ahead. Achieving a goal should not be seen as an endurance test: you will need stops and it may even be that you rest for a while at each stop, but you still have your map. You know the route and that deviating from it can be costly.

With all those thoughts in mind, enjoy …

It's your goal, you own it

Chapter 2
Identifying and clarifying

❏ Make your goal SMART:
  Specific
  Measurable
  Ambitious
  Realistic
  Timed

❏ Imagine your 80th birthday party

Most goals require a degree of hard work and focus. Some goals demand that you make changes, build new skills and take up challenges. It can feel scary, risky, or downright hard. But achieving your goal, no matter how great or small, will enhance your confidence and self-esteem and can potentially be nothing less than life-changing.

Identifying your goal

This probably sounds very simple – and perhaps it is! However, we want you to learn to be very specific and clear about your goal. Here is an example: Rebecca tells us, 'My goal is to lose weight.' We ask her to be more specific: add some words – be more precise, be clearer.

> Well, I want to lose about 2 stones and I want to keep it off – I'm fed up with dieting and then piling it back on. And I want to find a way to improve what I eat on a long-term basis without sacrificing enjoyment. I don't want to feel like it's all about denial for ever. It feels like food's my enemy but that can't be right.

So her specific goal is: 'I want to lose 2 stones, maintain my weight and learn more about good eating.'

You can see that there is quite a difference in stating the goal clearly. This will obviously affect the planning stage, which we will be looking at in much more detail in Chapter 7. With her specific goal Rebecca is starting to face up to the fact that she needs to behave differently with food. Like so many people she is caught in the diet-followed-by-weight-gain cycle. Dieting does nothing but take weight off, and Rebecca has realized she needs to become honest about what she does with food that causes her to regain the weight. She knows that if she does not stop that part of the cycle then she might as well not bother to diet! Rebecca is learning to be honest with herself and this will help her avoid the trap of magical thinking that often accompanies people trying to achieve their goals.

We are sure that you will understand what we mean by 'magical thinking' – this is when you do not really think your goal through or understand what steps need to be taken to achieve that goal. But you cannot leave things to chance or imagine that something 'magical' will happen to pull the goal together. You need to be in the driving seat at all times. Take charge and stay in charge – success tends not to happen by accident, but because it is made to happen. This is why it is so important to identify your goal and be specific about what you are trying to achieve. This makes you lay the cards out on the table from the outset and will help you later when you reach the planning stage. So remember that you will only reach your goals if you are absolutely clear about them, and are motivated, prepared, and in a can-do frame of mind.

Write down your specific goal.

Then ask yourself the following questions:

'Can I be more specific?'
'Can I describe it in more detail?'

Think about explaining your goal to a third person: you would have to outline every single detail to them. Be clear and concise.

■ Defining parameters and setting goalposts

Rebecca was our first example; let's now look at a second.

John's goal is, in his words, 'to get fit'. This is a great goal that tells us absolutely nothing; probably John doesn't feel very clear either. So we ask him to explain to himself what he really means. What is the 'picture' that he has of being or getting fit? What are the goalposts? What are the parameters, so that he has a yardstick to monitor his progress? This is such a key to maintaining motivation. In the business world you often hear people using the expression 'being SMART'. SMART is an acronym for:

▶ SPECIFIC
▶ MEASURABLE
▶ AMBITIOUS
▶ REALISTIC
▶ TIMED

Keep this word in your head at all times as you work on your goal.

John tells us:

> I'm 35 and get breathless if I have to run up steps. I'm not overweight, but I'm flabby and I suppose I know I don't look as good as I used to. If I'm really honest with myself I don't eat very well and I think I drink that bit too much.

We ask him to be specific. What is 'don't eat very well' and 'drink that bit too much'?

> I eat a lot on the run. I rush out of the house in the morning and grab a takeaway breakfast from a coffee bar – a danish or a croissant. Lunch tends to be sandwiches, or I sometimes go to the pub and get something with chips or a curry. In the evening I eat better because luckily for me my wife cooks and she usually makes chicken and vegetables or fish and vegetables.

We ask John what he specifically wants to change. (Remember that you have to be willing to make changes; change doesn't happen by magic and won't happen unless you decide that this is what you need to do). Being specific helps you get right to the core of what you are trying to achieve. John continues:

I like the food that I eat but I think it doesn't like me. What I mean by that is that I increasingly just don't feel particularly well and, as I say, I have probably gained 5–7 lb, which doesn't make me overweight, but doesn't make me look or feel good either. I would commit in my goal to 'get fitter' to:

1 Eat breakfast of toast or cereal and perhaps a piece of fruit before I leave the house.
2 Not eat sandwiches every day and, if I go to the pub, to have a salad or chip-free lunch, which I actually would enjoy.
3 Swim at least once a week at the weekend, as I enjoy swimming.
4 Take my son to the park and play football with him at the weekend – that will help my level of fitness as well as me giving him my time.

Oh, yes, on the subject of alcohol – I don't drink every day, but I probably have 4–5 pints of lager on a Friday and Saturday night. During the week I will have 1–2 pints at least two nights. When I drink on Friday and Saturday I always feel sluggish the next day. So my commitment with alcohol would be:

1 Have no more than one pint on a week night, and drink alcohol on no more than two week nights.
2 Not exceed two pints on a Friday and Saturday.

So you can see just how specific John has become. What he said also shows you some of the planning stage, just to give you an idea of what will come in Chapter 7. The key issue here is about identifying your goal and clarifying it. So John's desire to 'get fit' has developed into a goal that has structure. The important thing is to set goalposts or boundaries, adding quantities and time frames so that you give yourself something that you can start to measure your progress against. John now has lots of aims and goals within his goal, so that at the end of each week he can sit back and say, 'Yes, I am on target – I have done exactly what I have said I would do,' which helps build motivation.

Think about your parameters and goalposts. Think about time frames. Be specific at all times. Start right now by making some notes here:

We suggest that you make this your workbook or, if you prefer or need more space, keep a separate journal. Either way, keep a record of what you are doing and planning. This enables you to monitor your progress and keep yourself 'on track'.

Remember, no plan is a plan to fail.

■ Being realistic

This is a hard one, because goals are so subjective. What we don't want you to do is aim too low or high. In the next chapter we will be talking a lot more about getting motivated, and one of the things that Chapter 3 addresses is the need for you to be in a good and positive frame of mind when thinking about and working towards your goal. Aiming too high is obviously something to be wary of, but you must also be careful of aiming too low or dismissing a goal as impossible. You may be throwing away an opportunity to achieve something that could be incredible. One thing you can do if you are concerned about being unrealistic is to see if you can set some interim or 'micro-goals', as well as defining your final goal.

Take James, who at the age of 24 has decided that he wants to be a doctor. He does not have all the qualifications that he needs, and will have to do an intensive course to see if he can get two further science A-levels. Once he has done this he can then apply for medical school.

James flits from getting really excited about his goal to telling himself that he won't do it. We suggested that he took things one stage at a time and set micro-goals, which are the steps that will lead him to his final destination of qualifying as a doctor.

Stage 1 Apply to do intensive course.

Stage 2 Work towards exams and get feedback from tutors.

Stage 3 Apply to medical school after he's passed his A-levels.

James, like many people, has to decide how much he wants to try for the goal. He may be halted quite early on in the process and he has to have tremendous willingness to work very hard and take the risk to study subjects that he had steered away from. Successful completion of stages 1 and 2 would certainly give him the information that would tell him once and for all whether he was in a position to apply for medical school. Like many of us, he has a fear of failure, but we encourage everyone to give themselves permission to have a go. What does he really have to lose? Also, if he does not succeed it does not have to go to waste – it may be that he could use the experience and the knowledge that he has gained very profitably. He will also have achieved a lot in putting himself through various situations and, again, even if he didn't make his main goal, we don't feel he would have lost anything by trying.

Remember that you don't have a duty to succeed, but you should give yourself lots of affirmation and pats on the back for trying – that, too, is very important, so never forget it.

■ What's the core issue?

Cathy wants to change her job. We asked her to speak specifically about what she wants to move away from to help her identify her goal and to become clearer about it.

> I work as an administrative officer in a large corporation. I like what I do very much. I do quite a lot of keyboard work but I also make travel arrangements and organize small functions and dinner parties. I particularly love the corporate entertainment side and the travel side. I have, however, been thinking about leaving my job because I feel very isolated at work – I'd like to feel more part of a team

As Cathy continued to speak it sounded – and we are sure it sounds the same to you – as if there really is only one thing that makes her want to leave. She feels isolated and would like to work as part of a team, or feel that there is a team element to her work. The question that we put to Cathy was: 'Is it possible to achieve what you want, i.e., to work as part of a team, not by leaving your current job, but discussing your needs with HR [human resources]?'

We are not changing Cathy's goal – what we are doing is picking out the core issue. She has, until now, seen that the only solution is to leave the company rather than discussing it with human resources. The solution does not necessarily lie in talking to human resources, but the key point is identifying the core of the goal rather than unnecessarily changing something that doesn't need to be changed. In simple terms what we are saying is, 'Don't throw the baby out with the bath water!'

Finally, we ask Cathy to think about the consequences if she is going to discuss this with human resources.

▓ First things first

Angela wants to make some changes in her life that make us very concerned.

> I feel like a complete change. My goal is to sell my flat and move to London. I want to reinvent myself. I want that 'fresh start' that people talk about.

When we talk more to Angela, it isn't quite as exciting or positive as it sounds. We ask her why she wants a fresh start.

> Well, I've broken up with yet another boyfriend and I feel that my life is a mess. I am not really enjoying anything at the moment.

As we talk to Angela we come to realize that Angela is not just a bit fed up – she is actually quite depressed.

> I'm not sleeping well. When morning comes I don't want to get out of bed. I feel tired all the time. I am eating loads. I'm not interested in anything.

Angela has some classic symptoms that we feel she should discuss with her doctor. She is not in a healthy frame of mind to be making big decisions and we genuinely believe that making huge changes will not only stress her but will put her into a situation where she has no friends and no energy to restart her life.

All of us need to be in a good frame of mind and feeling physically well before we attempt to take on the challenge of making our goals a reality, something we talk more about in the next chapter in more general terms. Angela's example is something that we want to share with you because there will be people reading this book who are considering changes and setting goals for some very serious reasons that may be linked to depression, or are a result of a bereavement, trauma, eating disorder, addiction problem or family problem.

For people in these sorts of situations should not expect making a change to have a 'magical' effect. Achieving goals will not heal problems unless those problems are being dealt with. If you identify with Angela or you know from your doctor that you are depressed, then you need to recover from your depression: have that as your goal. We all need to be well to achieve our dreams and ambitions, and we should always put energy into taking care of ourselves. Likewise, if you have a problem with food, drugs, alcohol or gambling, don't try to paper over that problem by setting other goals. You would need to tackle those problems first because they will always contaminate what you are trying to do. Or, if you have a health problem, make it a priority to deal with that as effectively as possible. Don't set other goals as an avoidance tactic or as a way of de-focusing.

If you identify with anything that we have said in the last few paragraphs you may want to consider seeking further help. All we are asking is for you to be realistic and take care of yourself. Someone suffering from, say, depression could go to their doctor and be given help, through medication or therapy or both, and thereby be much better equipped to tackle their goals. Tackling goals while suffering from something like depression is truly a mountain to climb. Perhaps there's a medical problem niggling away or even causing serious concern. Ignoring something like that just uses up energy and depletes motivation – so goals aren't achieved and better health isn't achieved either. *Much better to seek the medical advice first.*

Owning your goal

Identifying and clearly stating your goal not only creates commitment and helps you start to work on a plan, but it also creates ownership and focus. So many of us do things 'by accident' or leave things to fate. Ask ten people you know how they got where they are today and the majority will say, 'Oh, I never planned this – it just sort of happened.' Some of these people may well be 'successful' in your eyes, but the amazing thing is that they never had their situation as a goal.

Owning your goal is a key ingredient in 'getting up and doing it'. If you don't identify your goal clearly and concisely and say to yourself, 'This is my goal – this is what I want to do,' then you never have the ownership that can be incredibly motivating. In a study at Harvard University business-school graduates were asked the following question: 'How many of you have clear, written goals and have made a plan to accomplish them when you leave Harvard?'

3 per cent had written their goals down

13 per cent had unwritten goals

84 per cent had no goals at all

Ten years later they met up at a reunion. The 3 per cent who'd written out their goals were earning, or were worth, ten times as much as the other 97 per cent. This is, of course, only one yardstick against which to measure success, but it is a pretty powerful one.

■ Self-limiting beliefs

Stating your goals and committing to them puts you in contact with choices. It also tells you something about how you view yourself. Write down three things that you have always wanted to do but haven't.

Leave a space to the right of each statement and write down in those spaces the reasons why you haven't done any of these things. These reasons will tell you a great deal about yourself. Firstly, it will tell you about what are called 'self-limiting beliefs', and tell us how we view our own capabilities.

Judith did this exercise:

1 I've always wanted to ride a horse
   I'm scared of hurting myself and I don't have time at
   the weekends

2 I've always wanted to go to India
   I just don't get round to saving up and I don't have a
   friend who wants to go

3 I've always wanted to speak French
   I was useless at school. I find it difficult to get myself
   organized to go to classes in the evening

Looking at Judith's wish list (it's a nice way to describe your goals), she is not asking to achieve anything that really looks impossible, but she does have some very definite limiting beliefs that stop her from seeing that she does have choices. The first thing we noticed was the issue of time, which is something everyone will recognize. The second is organization, which is probably a huge key. If Judith gets organized then she can probably make time and thereby make things possible. If she organized herself then she could start saving up to go to India – it doesn't matter how long she gives herself to do this. Thirdly, she limits herself by saying that she is going to hurt herself if she tries to learn to ride a horse (as horse riders we are certainly not disputing that you can hurt yourself!) but, again, she is focusing on that and assuming that an accident will happen. She also limits herself with studying French by saying that she was 'useless' at school. How can anyone get excited about doing something or believe in themselves if they view themselves as 'useless'? Judith is perfectly entitled to have a go at something like learning a language, and she doesn't have to be perfect or learn to speak like a native. Her personal best is good enough.

What we want you to do is to get into the driving seat with the map of the route you want to take in your hand and get your foot safely on the accelerator. Remember above all that there is no reason not to enjoy your journey – you've got your eye on the final destination, but have fun and savour every moment along the way.

■ Imagine your 80th birthday party

This is another great exercise to help you think about your goals — it may be that there are lots bubbling around as you think of your 80th birthday party. Imagine yourself at the last part of your life. Your family have thrown an 80th birthday party to celebrate your life and simply to show their love of you. You are asked to say a few words about your life. What would you want to say if you could choose the life that you would like to reflect back on? Again, this helps you look at the way you would like to see yourself, which in itself is important information, and also helps you think about the choices you would love to make.

Thomas made a great job of planning his 80th birthday party:

First of all I have to say that I look great! I have a perfect head of snowy white hair and I look fit – still nice and slim with a good straight back. It isn't a big party because I don't like large numbers of people, but I have my dear wife, my two children and my four grandchildren. My brother and sister are there with my nieces and nephew and their children. It's fantastic – all the people I care about are there and one or two old friends.

When I make my speech I'd certainly like to say how important my family has been and that to make a good husband, father and friend has been something that I feel proud of, and that I have invested a lot of time in people and have gained enormously from it. I'd also like to talk about my contribution to working with young people and working for charity. I have always felt that I would feel good about my life if I could look back and say that I have given something and as, I have said, I genuinely enjoy people and consider my relationships very important.

On a more selfish level I'd like to think that I had had a few adventures in my 80 years. I like travel and I suppose that I'd love to look back and say that I have travelled extensively – I'd certainly love to say that I have been to India, Africa, Australia and South America! They certainly would be goals that I'd love to achieve. (I am just finishing my training to be a solicitor so I'd like to look back and say that I was successful at work.) You won't be surprised to know that I want to do something with family law and that I hope to be able to make a difference to people's lives when they are probably at a very low ebb.

This chapter is a very important one for you to work on and think about. We cannot emphasize enough that to succeed you have to be SMART: Specific, Measurable, Ambitious, Realistic and Timed. It is absolutely no good to have a goal that is vague because you have nothing tangible to aim for. Being Specific also helps you at the planning and resourcing stage, and also leaves you prepared to face any hurdles or obstacles, as well as just making you very focused. If you are not focused you will easily lose direction and motivation.

M stands for measurable and, again, is about being specific, not only about your goal but in setting yourself time limits and time frames – we will talk a lot more about this in the chapters on planning (7 and 8).

Of course, you need to be Ambitious. Don't set your goal too low – you need to aim as high as possible and by doing that you are sending yourself a very powerful message: 'I can do this – I am capable.'

R is for realistic, which we have talked quite a lot about in this chapter: don't set unrealistic goals or try to do something when you are not well or have some serious problems that may need to be sorted out first.

T is for timed: set time limits and time frames to help keep you on track. They also give you an opportunity for positive feelings when you hit the targets you have set.

How thoughts drive feelings

Chapter 3
Getting motivated

❏ Your power source: feeding it, not depleting it

❏ The power of visualizing

❏ Tip the balance in your favour

This chapter is about teaching you some strategies that will help generate, increase and maintain your motivation. Motivation is a key ingredient in working on and achieving your goals. Think of it as an energy and power source – without it you will run of steam and find that you just lack that vital spark to keep going. But you need to be able to keep going, and silence doubt and negative messages. You also need watch out for old patterns that come into play and wrong-foot you before you even have time to realize what is happening. Most important of all, you need to have the energy and the right frame of mind to act – at all times – as if you will succeed.

As you work on improving and enhancing your energy sources, you must learn to be protective of them. We can all short-change ourselves by getting distracted or allowing our focus to wander. If you do unnecessary tasks or start to get depleted by worry and anxiety, you will use up that energy.

In the meantime, let's get you going by learning some up-to-the-minute strategies that will not only be useful as you work on your goal but also in your everyday life.

■ Seeing is believing

We would like you to do this short exercise. You have thought about your goal in Chapter 2 and have taken time to identify and clarify it. This chapter is about learning some things about yourself that will build into very useful strategies, as well as improving your motivations when you work on 'picturing', 'imagining' and, literally, 'seeing' your goal.

Here is an example. Sarah has been self-employed for a number of years. She has built up a very successful catering business but she has fallen into the trap of working incredibly long hours. Not only does she work long hours, she does many different jobs: all the administrative work, appearing at functions, placing the orders, etc. Sarah's specific goal is to work fewer hours. She intends to have two days off a week. She intends not to exceed 35 hours a week. She has decided that she will delegate certain parts of her work. (She has been very specific with the goal but we won't go into too much detail for the purposes of this exercise.)

We asked Sarah to sit down and think about her decisions and her goals and then to tell us what happens:

When I think about working fewer hours I feel a tremendous sense of relief and excitement. I can actually *see* myself at home doing 'normal' things that I miss – just watching television, talking to friends on the telephone, going to an exercise class – and I get really excited.

Then I go into my 'insecure head': 'Suppose I lose clients?' 'What about the money? – I'm going to have to pay someone to do some of the work that I have been doing.' When this happens I feel anxious and scared and the 'screen' goes blank: I don't see anything in my head, I just hear those thoughts in my head. It's a bit like a radio play.

One very important thing to take from Sarah's example is that when she was thinking positively, she actually 'pictured' herself, and this is obviously a very powerful tool to fuel her enthusiasm and positive feelings. On the other hand, when she began to think negatively she became more aware of an internal voice, which she likens to a radio play. So she switched from a television play, or a visual experience, to a radio play, which is an auditory experience. At the point she loses contact and motivation, her screen goes blank. She is no longer thinking about her goal, her motivation has gone, so there is nothing to move on towards.

Think about your own goal. Put this book down for a few moments while you do it.

When you have run through your own goal and your thoughts and feelings around it, ask yourself the following question: did you think about the positives or negatives first, or go from one to the other? Part of this process reflects your natural decision-making style. Once you have made a decision, however, you need to keep focusing on the positives, the reasons why you are doing what you are doing, and the benefits that achieving your goals will bring. The negatives don't have to be ignored – that would be ridiculous – but let them comfortably sit on the sidelines rather than giving them too much power.

To understand this strategy further you need to think about the following: some people favour the visual, some the auditory, some the kinaesthetic (feelings), and some, occasionally, the olfactory (sense of smell) when they are thinking about or recalling specific incidents. Some people are a mixture, but most people will favour one sense more than the other. If you tend not to favour the visual it is a good skill to develop because it is an excellent motivational tool.

■ Visual experiences

Do you think in pictures, i.e. do you see what you are thinking about? Are your thoughts almost like a video playing in your head or a series of still images as if you are flicking through a photograph album? If you identify with this, it means that you are a visual person.

Now think about your particular goal. Your goal might be, for example, that you want to become more assertive, so 'picture' a scene of yourself acting assertively. It may be that you think about returning a garment to a shop because it has developed a fault – the seam has split. In the scenario you will see yourself speaking to the shop assistant. You can also add volume to the 'video' and hear yourself being assertive when talking to the shop assistant.

Understand that being assertive means that you are clear about what you want, that you state this unambiguously and that you do it in a non-aggressive manner: So you might say: 'I would like you to replace this item or give me my money back. The seam of the blouse obviously was not stitched properly.' The assistant may try to argue, but you do not deviate from your goal and eventually you see yourself leaving the shop carrying a bag with a new blouse in it. When you play that video about achieving your goal of assertiveness, what do you notice?

We spoke to Alison, who has had problems with assertiveness, and her goal was to develop assertiveness skills. The above scenario was one that she wanted to be able to deal with. So, she played this scenario through in her mind and afterwards she had the following to say:

When I first 'saw myself' walk into the shop it felt very much like the old me. I was nervous – I actually felt the butterflies in my stomach. This type of situation has been one that I would dread or avoid because it very rarely went my way. Anyway, I was determined in my head that I am now armed with my new assertiveness skills because I have been on a course, so I got on with the techniques that I had learned. I started to feel excited and I also felt very determined. I also knew that I had done well on the course, so it was just a case of carrying out what I had learned. There really is a format: state clearly what the situation is and then state clearly what you want. Do not be aggressive, be polite. Well I just 'watched' myself do all of this and it felt great. I really felt excited – I really felt that I want to get out there and try it for real.

So Alison actually got to *see* herself being successful in her goal. On top of that she also got to *feel* the good feelings, the sense of excitement and the satisfaction of achieving her goal.

This exercise is a very powerful one in terms of getting motivated, as you get to sample what it will feel like. To do the exercise well you have to be willing to throw yourself into it, so don't be held back by scepticism. To do it properly you need to:

1 Be somewhere quiet where you won't be disturbed.
2 Close your eyes.
3 Think of the screen that you want to play the scenario on. It may be like a TV screen or, even better, a huge cinema screen.
4 Take your time to create the scenario: in the above example Alison would have needed to picture the store, etc., in detail.
5 Start the film rolling. Use your imagination – you would have been very good at this as a child. Did you not imagine yourself as a cowboy, Scarlett O'Hara or whatever? During childhood you would have day-dreamed and fantasized readily.
6 Project what you are seeing on to that screen. Really focus on you. See yourself doing whatever it is you want to achieve. Step inside that image and start to feel those positive feelings. They may be of excitement, pride, increased self-esteem, awe – the list is endless.

This is something you can keep doing to maintain your resolve – remind yourself at any time how good it will feel to achieve your goal. Remember to play that 'video' or 'film' often and see yourself achieving the goal. When the image is nice and big and bright, step into yourself on the screen and feel those wonderful feelings. Seeing really is believing.

■ Auditory experiences

You may be more of an auditory person or find that some of your thoughts and experiences are driven through the hearing senses. This may feel more like a 'radio play'. There may be no visual experience or there may be some. Remember that people can be a mixture, but perhaps tend to experience one sense more than the other. Remember also, as we said above, if you don't tend to 'picture' naturally it is a useful tool to get you and keep you motivated, so do keep practising it.

Mark certainly has a strong auditory side when he is thinking:

> I am genuinely very interested in words and like to listen to radio, so I don't know if that is why I often 'hear' words very strongly when I am thinking. When I am thinking about achieving my goal I literally can hear people talking to me about succeeding: 'Well, Mark, you've been a bit of a dark horse. How long have you had this up your sleeve? It's tremendous – fancy studying and completing an Open University degree and not telling anyone until you had finished!'
>
> There is a lot of that talk inside my head. I also do picture myself on graduation day – that is a very powerful image, but again I hear lots of things when I do picture myself. I also think about what I'd be thinking and saying to myself. *The sense of pride that I would have.*

So Mark's 'radio play' also consists of his own 'internal dialogue'.

■ 'Feelings' experiences (kinaesthesia)

Although people will tend to favour one sense more than another, there is bound to be a mixture of experiences as people play their goal through in their heads. One very powerful motivating force is to be able to *feel* the good feelings.

Let's take Paul as an example:

> To be honest I felt completely daft when asked to do this exercise, but when I practised it it really started to feel good, and I use the strategy a lot for lots

of different things. I was asked on this occasion to think and picture achieving my goal and to put it onto an imaginary screen so that I could see it and *feel* it.

My goal is to learn to ride a horse. I am a bit more challenged than most because I am 45 and I have even never sat on a horse before. It has been an ambition of mine for years – and of course people tend to laugh at me when I say it, or immediately tell me about famous people, like Christopher Reeve, who were nearly fatally injured in a horse-riding accident. I certainly don't make light of that, but all the same the fact that I don't get any enthusiasm from anyone else or any encouragement does tend to make it harder. I have to generate my own enthusiasm and I suppose there is also a part of me that is actually scared I might hurt myself. I think everyone falls off, so that is a certainty that I don't look forward to – in fact, it scares me.

Anyway, when I start to think about creating my own riding video I picture myself on a jet-black horse (it's probably Black Beauty!), and we are galloping through a huge field. The sun is shining and you can hear the rhythm of the horse's hooves on the earth. I imagine myself sitting on the horse and I think about how amazing that must be to be able to do that. I let myself hear the hooves striking the earth, and feel the sun on my back, I feel the wind in my face, then I try to imagine how exhilarating that would be, how exciting, what an achievement that would be – I try to feel those incredible feelings.

It does work – I actually find that the feelings of exhilaration and excitement that come up when I think about it make my heart beat faster! I suppose that's part of my goal, to be able to feel like that.

You must keep replaying those videos and radio plays. It is also important to emphasize that most people become exhilarated and excited when they think and talk about their goals. Unfortunately, this can turn into feelings of fear, anxiety and negativity, which is why you have to keep on playing the positive images. Don't take the good feelings for granted – you need to work on keeping them on a daily basis.

All of this is the start of a process that needs constant feeding; if you don't feed it, then nine times out of ten it will go nowhere.

One further point in terms of keeping your motivation going is that the process requires energy – don't try to do things when you are feeling tired, but try to take steps when you are feeling good and well-rested, as this will help you achieve your results.

■ Fighting FEAR

We will talk more about blocks to success in Chapter 4, but firstly there are two important issues to help keep you motivated and stop you from getting wrong-footed.

First, think about how your thoughts drive your feelings. This means that you must be aware of hurdles to positive thought at all times, a major one being fear, which can step in and push you off track. Secondly, you need to be protective of your motivation and you need to feed it, not deplete it.

Let us remind you of something: FEAR is an acronym for 'False Evidence Appearing Real'.

Think about that for a moment. If we feel fear about something in the future we often create the scenario, picture it or feel it as if it were real, or as if it were actually going to happen. Say, for example, you have made a serious mistake at work. You feel so awful that you go home rather than try to sort it out. You spend the evening at home worrying and start to get afraid of what will happen. You probably start to play certain scenarios through: 'Supposing I go to work tomorrow and get sacked? Supposing my boss tells everyone what I've done? Supposing this affects my bonus?' The list of projections is as endless as it is negative. All of this is 'false evidence', but it is so powerful that it will start to affect how you feel and, as a result, it influences what you do. None of it has happened, but it is affecting you now just as if it *had* happened. Think what this does to your motivation when working towards a goal.

This is a negative example of the visualization exercise that you have done. For anyone who says, 'Oh I can't imagine things that haven't happened,' think again – people are incredibly good at imagining the negative so realistically that they start to get all the feelings and thoughts associated with this thing that may never happen. Think again about the capabilities you have to imagine and create a picture, but this time consider how powerful it could be to use your imagination in a positive way.

Remember:

*Your thoughts drive how you feel: they can generate motivation
or destroy it.*

You can use them in a very positive way, as our exercise has shown, or they can generate fear that will get in the way of achieving your goal. If you are worrying about something that hasn't happened and may not happen, then you are using that 'false evidence' in a very destructive way. As you well know, your fears often do not become reality, but you can still be ruled by that fear. Start to develop more of a sense of the 'false evidence' that you collect that just ends up getting in your way.

Stop being influenced by something that has not happened.

Stop living in the dread of what 'may' happen and start to concentrate more on today, the only day you have any real influence over.

▧ Tipping the balance: a motivational strategy

To increase and generate motivation it is also important for you to understand the decision-making process. Once you understand what we naturally do you can use this as another strategy to propel you on your way.

Imagine an old-fashioned set of scales, the ones that have two brass cups suspended from the arm of the scale by chains. The process of making a decision is mirrored by these scales. As we start to think about a goal we begin to load the cups either for or against.

Geoff, a 30-year-old teacher illustrates this:

I have been thinking about changing my career for a while. I really know what I want to do – I want a career in IT (information technology). I am genuinely interested in this field. I also have a skill set that fits well with IT. Something else that embarrasses me is that I am drawn by the image – I feel that people have an image of male teachers that is a negative one. I am also really drawn by the financial rewards and career prospects – in one year's time I will be earning at least 15–20 per cent more than I am now and that will improve over time.

> Visualize the set of scales: one of the brass cups is being filled with all the reasons why this goal should be pursued and as it is filled it becomes heavier and starts to get lower and lower. At the same time the other cup starts to rise. This illustrates an expression we are sure you have heard, 'to tip the balance'.

Let's get back to Geoff.

There are probably other positive things that I think, but I can't think of any more at the moment. Anyway, you'd think that I had made my mind up, when I start to think of the positives of teaching. I don't mean that they come out in any order – they don't – but I think about things like the fact that I genuinely believe that I make a difference to the lives of the pupils I teach, not only academically, but also in a pastoral sense. I can be someone for them to turn to in times of trouble. I do get a lot out of that. I also love the holidays and use the summer to do some extensive travelling. I do have a lot of work to do outside school hours, but I'd imagine [in IT] that I will have less time to myself. [In teaching] I obviously don't have fears of redundancy – I know that I have to do a good job and I pride myself that I do – but I certainly don't fear that my job will go because of a change in market forces, so I suppose I have security.

> Look what is happening to the set of scales: that cup that was so high in the air has become fuller and fuller and has started to draw level with the other one as its weight counterbalances it. If you visualize this well you can see Geoff getting really motivated by his goal and then talking himself out of it by loading the scale on the other side. This is not a bad thing – it is about exploring for 'fors' and the 'againsts'. In this book we don't encourage anyone to do anything without thinking it through. Looking at Geoff's set of brass cups we would imagine that at the moment things are probably finely

balanced, which means that making the decision is difficult. There is a lot he loves about his current job, and he can't ignore that because he has to live with the consequences, but he won't achieve his goal unless he throws all his energy into it.

Another exercise you can do if you are having problems making up your mind is to write down the *fors* and *againsts*. If your goal involves choosing one thing over another you could, instead, divide a piece of paper in two and write all the fors for both scenarios and compare them. You could then move on to do a list of againsts and compare those.

Let's do that with Geoff's example:

TEACHER	IT
For	**For**
Makes a difference	Skill-set match
Personal satisfaction	Career prospects
Holidays/travel	Image
More time outside work	Finance
Job security	
Against	**Against**
Image	Less secure
	Less time outside work
	Shorter holidays
	Not making a difference

For   _Against_

For _Against_

Geoff may eventually tip the balance by thinking about what really drives and motivates him. There seems to be a lot about teaching that looks positive, but if he is truly driven by finances and image then IT will probably win over. However, if issues like 'making a difference' are most important to Geoff, then IT would probably not be such a good fit. In Chapter 7, which covers planning, we will be talking to you about the kinds of goals that you really need to research. Perhaps someone like Geoff should invest in a visit to a careers consultant, who can spend an entire day looking at his strengths and assets and advise on what truly fits him career-wise.

It's a good idea to look back at this exercise when you have read Chapter 6 and understand more about 'drivers'.

▓ Getting mentally fit

This chapter has demonstrated how our thoughts drive our feelings, and has also touched on the need to be in the right frame of mind as you set your goal. You need to be in the right mood, with good energy levels.

Understanding positive and negative effects is an important basis to success in goal-setting. Most goals require a good degree of energy to achieve them. Let's be really clear about this: don't balk at striving for a goal because it starts to feel like hard work – it *is* going to be hard work and, if it isn't, then you have probably chosen a pretty easy and straightforward goal. It follows that you should be aware of your energy levels – physically, mentally and emotionally – at all times, and avoid trying to do certain things when your energy is low. It would be like trying to do a marathon when you are developing flu, which would feel impossible and just simply too much. Remember that goals are very subjective, so to maintain your levels of motivation you have to keep *feeling and telling yourself* that the goal really is attainable. Remember also that fear of failure, which is a protective mechanism, will constantly try to do battle with the feelings of optimism and that 'can-do' frame of mind that you are building.

In this chapter we have talked about sharpening up thought processes and have mentioned a little about being aware of your physical as well as mental state. Later on in the book we will expand on what we call the 'whole-person concept' (pages 78–82), a major tool in achieving your goal. To conclude this chapter we want to leave you with some thoughts about your environment.

Beechy and I went to do a presentation in a huge investment bank some years ago. What struck us was the opulence of the building and the amazing marble columns and incredible wood floor and panelling. The building was wonderfully cool on a very hot summer's day. Noise was minimal and everything smelled of furniture polish and the scent of the beautiful lilies we placed on the shiny mahogany tables.

There has been a great deal of research done into the effect of environment on workers' moods. Not many of us have the opportunity to work in the environment we've just described, but we can emulate some of the key ingredients. An environment that is well-organized, uncluttered, as physically pleasant as possible, with nice smells, and so on, is all-important and will undoubtedly affect our moods. Say, for example, that you go to a particular place when you are working on or thinking about your goal. Perhaps you use a corner in a bedroom as a study, or the garden shed – it doesn't matter. What does matter is that it is organized, quiet and as pleasant as possible.

In a wider sense the more organized you are in general, keeping your home as uncluttered, tidy and as pleasant as possible, the more you will contribute to a feeling of motivation and the 'right frame of mind'. Do not take your frame of mind for granted – you need to nurture it, preserve it and work on it.

Staying in touch with reality

Chapter 4
Blasting blocks

❑ The gremlin exercise

❑ Your bill of rights

❑ Identify the anchors that keep you in one place

❑ The whole-person concept

Think of every time you have said to yourself: 'I couldn't do that,' 'I couldn't possibly attempt that,' 'I'd only fail,' 'It's not worth it,' ' I couldn't take the disappointment of failing,' 'Other people would be better at it,' or 'I wonder what I am doing even thinking about this?' If you had a diamond for each time those thoughts have occurred to you, we wonder how big the necklace would be! If we were to take a guess, we would say that it probably would be very big, because most of us say so many things to ourselves that can stop us from going forwards. These things stop us from realizing our potential, and therefore stop us from realizing our dreams, hopes and ambitions.

▓ Being aware of self-sabotage

There are lots of different ways you can sabotage yourself and the awful thing is that sometimes it won't even feel as though you're doing it. It can be so subtle. You may be reading this and thinking, 'What are they going on about sabotage for? I don't do that.' Well, it may be that you think you don't do it because you simply don't notice. It has probably become such an integral part of that negative self-talk that goes on inside your head that you really aren't aware of it. As we warned you in the introduction to the book, you need to watch out for sabotage. You need to start noticing because it can come from anywhere, such as inside you, or sometimes from other people, and it can be very well disguised.

▓ How other people can sabotage you

Remember that not everybody around you will want you to change as a result of your goal. Other people can feel threatened when you start to make changes. Perhaps you are doing something that they would love to do, but they can't, or maybe they feel that you will change and become different towards them. It could be that they are used to manipulating you, or that a problem you seek to resolve through your goal will mean you won't need them in the way you have before.

Now, we are not saying that your friends or your partner are bad people, but some people behave like this because deep down inside all of us we want things to be the way that *we* want them to be. Generally, when you are involved with other people you will want them to do things the way you like them done.

So when someone around you makes some changes and starts doing things differently and says, 'I'm not doing that any more – I don't think it works and I want to do it this way instead,' it can come as a shock and feel threatening. This is also an example of an assertive change in someone. Perhaps this person has never been assertive before, but now they have changed, and people around them are going to react, more often than not, in a negative or bewildered way: 'What's happened to them?' If they hear a 'no' from someone who has never really said it before, they are likely to interpret it as 'being difficult', 'being argumentative' or 'being defiant'. But that 'no' is none of those things: it is about being honest and saying, 'I don't want to do it this way any more.'

Here is an exercise that will really help you examine just how much you can sabotage yourself and how people throughout your life can have given you 'messages' that have left you feeling very negative. One of the keys is to begin to 'notice', and this is what this exercise achieves:

■ The gremlin exercise

This might sound fun, but this exercise actually packs a real punch if you sit down and work through it. We all know what a gremlin is, and we all have one – if you like, it is that negative part of us. It can be made up of – or these can contribute to it – our negative thoughts and experiences, and negative things that people have said or done to us throughout our lives. We have already talked about positive and negative self-talk, and this is an exercise for you to stop and think some more about a side of you that you need to continue to 'tame'. That's why this exercise is called 'taming your gremlin'. Think about:

1 The negative things you say to yourself, e.g., 'I'm useless,' 'I'm no good at learning,' I'd never be a…'
2 Key people in your life – teachers, classmates, friends, parents and family – who have said negative things to you that have really stuck, for example if your teacher said, 'You'll never come to anything,' or a parent said, 'Who do you think you are?'. etc.
3 Things in your life that have affected the way you feel about yourself, e.g., if you were bullied at school.

4 Whether you have very set reactions to certain things, almost as if you are programmed.

Your answers are useful pieces of information that the 'gremlin' feeds on, because it is the negative side of you – the side that doubts yourself, has low self-esteem and lacks confidence. What you need to do is to stop 'feeding' the gremlin. Instead, starve him by learning to be more positive with yourself and also understanding where some of your negative thoughts and messages come from. When you can understand why, rather than assuming 'that's just me', you can get a sense of power from being able to change some of these things.

Sabotage from yourself and others are two of the blocks to your way ahead, and to help you blast some more blocks we are presenting your 'Bill of Rights' below. This is a personal bill and is a very important list for you to learn and be aware of. If you look at the Bill of Rights here most of you will identify areas that you struggle with or don't really believe are your right. Or you may have the belief, but struggle to put it into action.

■ A bill of rights

To start blasting the internal blocks that we have created we need to give ourselves permission to do the things in the list below.

We all have the right to:

Be treated respectfully
Be listened to and to be heard
Ask for what we need
Change our minds
Take responsibility if we make the wrong decision
Make mistakes
Choose to 'let things go'
Say 'no'
Say 'yes'

> Ask for help
> Voice our opinion, whether it is right or wrong
>
> Many people tend to be compliant and will say, 'Yes,' and, 'Of course,' but
> inside the dialogue is different: 'Why do I have to do this?' or 'Why can't I
> say what I mean?' So many people never speak out until reading this page
> in this book. It is time for you to find your inner voice.

Removing negative blocks

One of the first things that you need to do is gain a greater sense of awareness, and a most effective way of doing this is for you to make a list of the ways you block yourself from doing different things. I use the word 'block' and Josephine uses the word 'anchor', which is a really good metaphor, because we understand that when a ship drops its anchor that boat is going nowhere – it is stuck. Our blocks are just like that. We believe that we can't move them – or that is how it feels. Well, we *can* move them, but initially that won't feel possible. At the moment they are stopping you from getting to your goal: your goal of success, of breaking these negative patterns and of feeling good. Remember that the way you feel drives the way that you feel. Let me say that again: 'the way you feel drives the way you feel'. If you are feeling good then you are going to get your goals. By attaining those goals you are going to feel good about yourself. If that sounds like a strange thing, think back to the last time that you really felt good about yourself on an ongoing basis.

Someone once said to us that 'continuity breeds success'. If we can keep the continuity of moving forward, the goals become closer and then we attain them along with a new form of self-worth. And that is what we are after, 'the worth of you'. Remember that the only competition you have is yourself. Let go of trying to be like other people: while you are doing that you are not really achieving your own potential. Too many people are running around trying to be like everybody else. What about your own individuality? What about the special talents that you have? You may sit and grimace, 'What special talents are they going on about?', but everyone is an individual with their own talents. You have to start treating yourself as if you are very, very special: this in itself will help you start to blast those blocks.

▓ Identifying your anchors

Remember that achieving your goal will be a lot less taxing if you are not sabotaging yourself. So, ask yourself what your anchors might be and make a list of them. Let us help you with a few of them. Say, for example, you want to change your job: you might be held back by the 'velvet handcuffs' anchor – i.e., a big salary, good holidays, perks such as healthcare insurance or a pension. While that might look good on paper, the key question is, are you happy in your job?

A good question to ask yourself in any situation is, 'What is it really costing me to stay?' By this we mean that you should ask yourself questions like:

1 How much of my time do I spend feeling angry about work?
2 Does this spill into my leisure and home time?
3 Can I remember a time when I was far happier?
4 Do my long hours outweigh the financial gain, even if I have a large salary? Is it worth damaging myself for money? We remember a very worn-out executive friend of ours saying that if he were rushed to A & E with a heart attack, there would be no way he'd say, 'I'd do it all again.'
5 What is all this 'costing' me?

You can end up staying in a job for the big salary and perks, even though isn't giving you the fulfilment that you really need. One of the human needs that we cannot escape is to feel a sense of fulfilment and achievement. It obviously comes in very different shapes and forms, but it is something that cannot be overlooked. If it is, we put ourselves at risk.

Also watch out for perfectionism (see more on this below) and the unrealistic expectations anchors: they can set you up to fall flat on your face. We often say to people that the number-one cause of stress is 'reality' for those of you who are not in contact with it. Just read that sentence one more time to make sure that you have understood what we have said.

To avoid stress you have got to stay in touch with reality.

Don't set your sights too high, but set them just high enough so that you can see them and tell yourself that you are going to get there. Don't stress yourself by building a mountain and feeling defeated before you've even started.

Let's look at some key anchors in more detail.

▓ The patterns and habits anchors

As human beings we are creatures of patterns and habits, which are tremendous anchors. We tend to have habits that are very repetitive and, when you are always doing something the same way, you can fall into the trap of saying, 'This is how I've always done it,' and, 'I'm not going to try to do it any other way.' Part of getting stuck into a pattern is that it is familiar and is therefore very comforting. Well, if that isn't a tremendous piece of sabotage, we don't know what is! Nothing breaks habit like habit, so you have to work hard at creating new, positive habits, but this is entirely possible.

▓ The perfectionism anchor

'I can only do it if I do it perfectly' is another very powerful anchor. The truth is that we don't really do things perfectly, and that is actually okay. Keep telling yourself that it is okay to do the best that you can. Also, don't compare yourself to others. We talk about using other people as blueprints (in Chapter 6), but we don't have to do things exactly like other people. We need to be ourselves and to give ourselves credit for our achievements and what they say about us. Comparing yourself to others can leave you with feelings of inferiority. Trying to be a perfectionist is setting yourself up to fail, or it sets you up to think about things and then dismiss them, because you know that you are not going to reach your ideal. Perfectionism is a hindrance, because if you are a true perfectionist then nothing is ever good enough.

▓ The guarantees anchor

We would all, very understandably, like a guarantee, as it gives us an amazing sense of security – 'I can try this because I will succeed' – but that is not reality. If the lack of a guaranteed outcome is stopping you from making changes, you need to rethink. There will be a lot of you who have goals for which there is no guarantee. Unfortunately, life is not like a scientific experiment: we don't live in a controlled environment and we need to learn to deal with the unknown.

We are not encouraging you to be reckless, but we always say that you must be aware of the consequences of your decisions and actions, and you must be willing to take the outcome. You will be more in charge of the outcome than you give yourself credit for, so don't be afraid to give things your best shot. Moving forward is always positive, regardless of whether or not you know exactly what the end result will be. Making changes and doing things differently will open up opportunities that you would be unlikely to encounter if you keep to your familiar pattern. Even if things don't go according to your plan, you might still be very satisfied with the result.

▨ Responsibilities, duties and time restrictions

Practical issues such as your responsibilities, duties and time restrictions are three things that really can hold you back – 'I can't do that; I've got responsibilities,' or, 'I don't have time,' or, 'There are other things that I must put first.' If you don't want to break these patterns, then give this book to someone else. You must be prepared to take a different route. We are not telling you to ignore your responsibilities, but we are saying that you must not let them become something you may end up resenting later in life. Also, doing something for yourself does not mean that you are choosing one part of your life over another. There are a lot of very responsible people who take care of their families and also achieve their goals. You've probably been walking down this old road for a long time and it has been taking you nowhere. That is why you are reading this book.

▨ The fear and anxiety anchor

You've seen this acronym earlier in the book, but just let us remind you:

F ALSE
E VIDENCE
A PPEARING
R EAL

We fill ourselves full of fear, but most of it is constructed by us. As you know, 'false evidence' can appear so real that we start believing it and tell ourselves that we can't do something. Then, when we attempt to do it, we go against that fear that has been constructed and start to feel very anxious. The fear creates the anxiety and the anxiety creates more fear – it is an organic thing. Fear and anxiety are a very bad marriage. Together they act to be probably the biggest anchors of all. Start realizing how much fear you fill yourself with and how much anxiety that causes. It is powerful, very destructive and also very controlling.

The no-luck anchor

This is the 'if I was the only one in a raffle I still wouldn't win anything' anchor. We are sure you know exactly what we mean – it is almost like a superstition. It can feel to some of you as though it is a done deal: 'I'm not lucky and that is the end of it – there is nothing I can do to change it.' You will even hear people say that they come from an 'unlucky family'.

Think about what this message does to you and how much it influences the decisions you do make and those you don't. You are also telling yourself through this anchor that you have no choice, no responsibility and no influence. You are undermining yourself and telling yourself that there is something wrong with you, almost as if you are tainted.

From now on you need to believe that you can make your own luck. You are more in charge than you are giving yourself credit for, and there is no real reason why you shouldn't act like a winner.

The clutter and disorganization anchor

The physically tangible anchors such as clutter and disorganization can have a powerful mental impact. If we are untidy on the exterior, we can be untidy with our thinking. We can be unproductive with our time management and poor at maintaining a good work–life balance. These are serious anchors that can really hold us back.

If you recognize these as part of the way you are sabotaging yourself, then get these on to your personal 'to do' list and start being more aware of them.

The no-solution anchor

This is one of our favourite ones, not because we think it is funny or anything like that, but because we hear it so many times and we have the joy of watching people's faces when they start to become aware that there are solutions. However, we are not suggesting that all solutions are particularly obvious, or necessarily easy to implement or face. When people feel stuck they say things like:

> 'Stay with the familiar.'
> 'Everything is all right the way it is – I don't need to change anything.'
> 'I don't have to attain new goals.'
> 'There isn't a solution, so I won't try any more.'
> 'There is nothing that can be done.'
> 'I'm not even going to try – it's not worth it.'

Well, perhaps you will have to face change when you confront the 'no-solution anchor'. Remember the saying, 'Keep doing what you do and you will just keep getting more of the same.' If what you have is okay for you, then you don't really need this book. You already have it all!

The can't-see-the-future anchor

We are always projecting: 'Well, if I win the lottery at the end of this week I'll retire.' You are even projecting that you will still be alive at the end of the week! Having said this, we are surprised at how, when we ask people to imagine the future, they promptly tell us that they can't and yet they can easily make statements like the above. As we have already shown in Chapter 3, 'seeing' and 'visualizing' are key parts to achieving your goal and you need to be working hard on this.

The mountains anchor

'Oh just look at the task ahead – look at the size of this. I'll never be able to climb this. We'll never get over this.' A climb can be made in stages, and it is exactly the same with your goals. If a goal feels too great, break it down into manageable chunks. Later in the book (Chapter 8) we will talk more about creating micro-goals, which help counteract the 'mountains anchor'. If necessary, you can also make a weekly list of what to do to begin to tackle the goal. Don't be put off by the work ahead or the time it will take – just do it bit by bit. So don't try to climb the mountain all in one go. Set yourself tasks that are possible to complete. Make them realistic so that you don't put yourself off before you have even set out.

▓ The security-at-any-price anchor

Here is another anchor to be very aware of: 'If I have security, then everything will be okay and I'm just going to stay here.' Well that is just like saying, 'I'm going to stay stuck no matter what the consequences.' It is as though we sell our souls for security, isn't it?

We are not saying that security doesn't matter – of course it does. It is a very important aspect of people's lives. Everybody has a need to feel secure, and we should attend to that in a healthy way. What we are saying is don't let that misguide you, so that you can't expand your horizons or do things differently. You don't have to give up your security in order to effect change.

▓ The stress anchor

Because change is stressful it is so often mistaken as a warning sign not to proceed: 'Oh, it doesn't really matter whether I don't attain that goal, because it is causing me so much stress.' We believe that making positive change is naturally accompanied by some stress, which should not be confused with negative kinds of stress, such as the kind people feel when they have lost their sense of direction in life. We truly believe that people can enjoy working very hard when they see a point to it.

Also, let's lighten up here – it doesn't have to be all doom and gloom. If you are going to see this as really, really hard work and are not going to enjoy achieving your goals, then you are going to make it ten times as hard for yourself. Remember, every step you take towards a new goal is a positive step forward for you that will impact on all other parts of your life. Don't be so fearful about stress – hard work is not stress, and hard work can bring some wonderful things into your life.

Take some time to write down the thoughts you've had about the anchors that might be holding you down.

The whole-person concept

It is very easy to settle into a negative way of thinking, behaving and living. You can easily find yourself not taking care of yourself in various aspects of your life – physically, emotionally, mentally, socially and spiritually. We call this way of looking at people the 'whole-person concept' and it is important that we take care of ourselves in this rounded and whole way. Now, this sort of language may sound strange to you because this is not 'everyday' language. In our everyday life people don't ask questions like, 'Are you taking care of yourself physically, emotionally, mentally, socially and spiritually?' That doesn't happen and would sound bizarre if it did! This is a personal journey you're on – an 'inside job'. It's for you and no one else. It might affect and impact on other people, but they are likely to feel the benefits of you looking after yourself too.

Physical health

As we have said earlier in the book, you need to be in the best frame of mind and in the best of health in order to attain your goal. Ask yourself, first of all, if you are making the most of yourself physically. Are you showing care and respect for your body? Sadly, there will be a lot of you reading this who will probably want to skip this section rather than confronting the fact that you are not taking care of yourself. Beechy uses himself as a good example of someone who really didn't take care of himself in any sense of the word:

> One of the best decisions that I ever made in my life, other than giving up drinking, was to start to look after myself physically. It was something that I had never really done before because when I was drinking and taking drugs it was hardly something that I'd have done. It's pretty obvious that I just didn't care about myself. At that time I was caught up in a destructive pattern, and caring for myself did not feature. So, for me, late in my life, being physically active was really a big commitment. Josephine actually started exercising first and got herself a personal trainer and worked out three times a week. I realized one day that I was jealous of her progress. I remember looking at my waist and it was

getting bigger and bigger – that middle-age spread. Then I'd walk past paper shops and see the health magazines with guys with washboard stomachs. Yes, they were younger but they also represented something that is possible to some degree. It put me in contact with what I wasn't doing. I started slowly and have built up to running three to four times a week and using weights. Small change really does mount up!

I used my compulsive nature to the positive. I realized that exercise has changed how I feel and has had a huge impact right across the board. We both feel that it has been a major block-breaking thing to do. Exercise is so important if you are sitting down all day, as we do.

Exercise increases the endorphin and serotonin levels in your brain, which are naturally occurring chemicals that make you feel good. As you know, if you feel good then you will perform well, at your true potential. This has an incredible impact: it makes you feel good about yourself and as though anything is possible. This is key to that 'can-do' frame of mind that we keep talking about. So, ask yourself as you are reading this when the last time you felt really good about yourself was. We would challenge you that it was probably some time ago, unless you are one of the small number of people who exercise and look after themselves.

We can't say this strongly enough: do not dismiss taking care of yourself physically. If you are currently very unfit and have never been particularly fit you have absolutely no idea what the benefits are. Sadly, you will probably convince yourself that it couldn't happen to you, or you will allow yourself to be held back by fear of hard work. Start thinking about the rewards and stop focusing on what you call 'hard work' – it really will be life-enhancing.

Beware that the body betrays – you need to take care of yourself now. It is a machine and it does wear down and wear out. If you want to reach a potential that you have probably absolutely no idea you possess, physically you have to take action. Lots of people also fall into the trap of doing some exercise but not eating well. We don't talk too much about 'diets', but what you need to do is to follow a sensible eating plan. A lot of people eat far too much of what's not good for them and too little of what is. Think about it this way: you need to manage your food rather than being managed by it. If you exercise at the same time you will get that healthy balance and as a result, you will look good as well as feeling good about yourself. You can't get away from the fact that we all enjoy looking our best. You don't have to look like a stick to look good – it is important to accept the way your body is and not fall into the trap of starving to reduce a part that won't shrink. Women are particularly prone to going into battle with themselves rather than working on improving what they have.

You need to look after yourself through your diet and exercise, and understand that this is an investment for the future. There are many good books on these subjects from which to take your pick.

Emotional health

Your emotional health is all-important to your wellbeing. You should aim for an ability to feel and express feelings and feel the highs and the lows, but not be governed by them. Stay in touch with reality. Remember what we said before about reality being the number-one cause of stress for those who don't stay in touch with it. The way to stay in touch with reality is by being emotionally in touch with yourself. Look at your resentments and the way you feel about things. Ask yourself, 'Do I express my anger? Am I honest with people? Do I really tell them how I feel?' We know that you can't always tell people how you feel because sometimes it isn't appropriate and can cause unnecessary pain or upset. But be as honest as possible. Keeping your 'back yard' clean is going to keep your emotional house in order, and that is going to help you stay well.

Mental health

Your mental health is obviously very important, but most people's attitudes to mental health are drastically different from their attitudes to physical health. The reasons are so obvious – there are shame and fear, as well as ignorance around mental-health issues. We tend to take good mental health for granted and assume that 'it will never happen to me'. The reality is that we are all at risk of problems that will impact upon our mental health: none of us are immune and some are more at risk because there may be more of a predisposition. Depression, for example, has to be one of the most misunderstood illnesses, and this really can strike anyone – there is no profile of someone who is destined to be depressed or a profile of someone who would never become depressed. We believe, therefore, that you should watch the expectations you place on yourself in terms of the hours you work and how you deal with areas of your life that stress or worry you. It really is not a weakness to say, 'This is getting too much,' or, 'I need help – I can't find a solution that makes me feel better.'

We also believe that to be mentally well you need to be as open and honest as you can. As we said earlier on, we are not suggesting that you walk around insulting people or being unfair or unkind. There are degrees of openness and honesty that leave other people's feelings intact. We also think that one of the great dangers to mental health is when people do things that they fundamentally disagree with. This has to be something profound to have a major impact, but we have often worked with people whose life decisions have made them ill because they have broken a code that is very important to them.

Be true to yourself and that keeps you well.

Don't be one of these people who halts their progress by saying, 'That is far as I can go.' Remember this book is about getting up and doing it, reaching some dreams. It is so important to have dreams. People who are mentally fit have a great capacity to think and dream, and from those dreams an exciting reality can grow. Native Americans believe that we can become what we dream – so dream a good dream.

The social side

We are human and that means that we need to love and be loved. We need to develop and maintain meaningful relationships. Just take a moment to ask yourself:

How good am I at relationships?
How much am I able to love?
How much am I able to let myself be loved?

How good am I at accepting compliments?

How good am I at giving affirmation to others?

Do you prioritize relationships or do you allow work to dominate? Individual fulfilment can be very much a tug of war between two conflicting needs – our need to achieve and our need for relationships. Remember, we can be very good at thinking about what we need, but we also need to think about what other people need – it's a give-and-take process. You know how you feel about people who are self-centred and only think of themselves, so be careful not to become one of those people. Having the ability to be both 'other-centred' as well as being 'willing to receive' is so important in helping you develop and maintain meaningful relationships.

The spiritual side

Last but not least: spirituality. We believe that this is a very personal and magical part of our make-up. It is very important for us as human beings to have and be in contact with our spiritual values. Spirituality means lots of different things to different people, and many people confuse it with religion, which it is not. To us, spirituality is the ability to be in touch with whatever gives your life meaning, to have the choice to believe in a god or a higher power. It is important to have something to relate to – it doesn't have to be religious, but must be something that can give you strength in times of trouble, loneliness, despair or isolation, times when you really need something to hold on to.

Think about the spiritual side of yourself and explore the values that are important to you.

That is the whole-person concept. If you can work on all the different aspects – physical, emotional, spiritual, mental and social – that will help you have a really good balance within yourself. That balance will help you have the clarity to make decisions and the strength to face the fears that have been holding you back from attaining your goals. Above all, it is going to help you break down the blocks that hide away inside you, which have been stopping you from moving forward. Remember that actions speak louder than words, so let's start putting some of the things we have been discussing in this chapter into action. There is no point sitting and thinking about it – you have to get up and do it, like the title of the book. If you don't, you're going to stay stuck, and that is just not good enough.

Remember that life is a journey. You've probably noticed how quickly the journey is going. Just think back for a moment to when you were eight or nine years old. Does it feel that long ago? Look at how quickly the time has gone. Look at how quickly the years have gone by. We don't have time to wait. We really, really do have to get up and do this. Enjoy the journey, enjoy the changes, and enjoy the goals you are going to achieve and that, above all, you deserve to achieve.

Let's start – right now – blasting those blocks out of the way.

How well do you know yourself?

Chapter 5
Knowing yourself:
a personal inventory

❑ A day in the life – teach someone to be you for a day

❑ Make a detailed inventory of yourself

Not only do you need tools to help you 'get up and do it', but you also need as much insight as possible to help you prevent problems along your way. In Chapter 1 we focused upon the normal feelings people have about change and about pursuing goals.

Chapters 2 and 3 have helped you identify your goal and introduced some motivational strategies. Chapter 4 has helped you start to 'blast the blocks' that can cause you to grind to a standstill or completely give up.

This chapter is about taking time getting to know yourself. That sounds strange, doesn't it? Of course, we all know ourselves, but the depth of that knowledge and the attention to detail can always be improved upon. This chapter will obviously help you continue to blast blocks, but will also help you identify your plus points, your negative points, and your likes and dislikes. It will also help you discover any aspects of your life that are likely to get in the way of your goal, or whether your mindset needs careful examination. To put it another way, you will find out if the motivation behind your goal is something healthy and considered, or whether you are basically trying to escape the way that you feel or a painful situation.

To help you get to know yourself we will take you through the personal inventories of two different people with two very different goals.

We are going to meet Louise, who is 35 and wants to lose weight, and Simon, who is 32 and wants to change his job.

■ A day in the life: teach someone to be you for a day

This is a great exercise. Not only can it be fun, it is illuminating if you take the time to do it well. For the purposes of this book the 'day' should be influenced by the goal that you have set, so ensure that you are 'teaching' someone else about the issues relevant to the goal that you have set. Describe your day as fully as possible, as if you are literally explaining to a third party, and think of the questions they would ask, so that they can understand what it is like to be you. This is not a mad as it sounds, as it will ultimately help you become aware of the processes, thought patterns, habits and behaviours that you experience throughout your day. It will also help you see if your goal is one that comes out of desperation or unhappiness, or one that is well thought-out and not a 'universal cure-all' for your problems. Your third person does not have to be imaginary – if you have a trusted friend, you may even want to share this exercise with them. Get your friend to ask you as many questions as necessary so that they can explain back to you exactly what you do.

Louise

I have to say initially I found the idea ludicrous to teach someone to be me for a day, but when I started I realized that it made me focus and helped me look at my patterns with food.

My goal is to lose weight. To be specific, I want to lose 3 stones. That will bring me down to a comfortable weight. I won't look like a model, but I will be able to wear clothes that I like and I'll be able to enjoy tennis again and not feel out of breath and self-conscious. My goal is also about admitting that I have to change my eating habits. Usually, I lose weight, feel great and then just put it all back on again and some more.

I can't imagine that it will be easy to take weight off and, to be honest, I see my weight loss as something that is not permanent. Oh, what a negative message – I can see that now! It's true, though. I don't see it as a permanent thing – in fact, in terms of me projecting, if I'm really honest, I do think about the day I stop dieting and think about all the great things I'm going to eat. And by 'great' I mean chocolate, chips and things like that!

Okay, so I'm Louise and I'm 35 years old. I have two children who are both at school. Clare is seven and Sam is five. My husband is John and he is 39 and is a teacher. I wake up at 6.30 because the house is very chaotic in the morning. I have to leave the house by 8.15 to get the children to school and John likes to leave by 7.45, and he likes us to have breakfast together as he sees so little of the children during the week.

So I get up at 6.30 because I hate rushing. I am an organized person, so I tend to ensure that the children's school bags are packed and their clothes and gym things, etc, have been got ready the night before. That does make evenings very hectic, but I wouldn't be able to stand it any other way. When I go downstairs I have also already set the table and I tend to make myself a cup of tea and I usually nibble something. A bad habit is my liking for biscuits. I will often say I'll just have a couple of plain ones with my tea but it often ends up as many more. I also tend to munch the children's cereal and will pick it dry out of the packets. I do tend to feel tired in the mornings and feel I have a lot to get done in a short time (like loads of mothers!), but I do get genuinely very weary. What I now realize is that I do dwell on what I need to do – I fill that mental screen with lots of images of what needs to be done and I think I probably make too much of it. I exhaust myself before I've even got started.

I then eat toast and cereal. Usually two slices of toast with marmalade and an unsweetened cereal with milk. I also have two to three cups of tea. If the children leave anything I tend to nibble bits of leftover toast. I do seem to be using the word 'nibble' rather a lot! Then it's off on the school run – I just leave the dishes, etc, and get in the car. It's a tedious journey because the traffic is bad, but I enjoy the time with the kids – we tend to chat and sing, so it's quite a happy event.

After leaving them at school I'll go to the supermarket if I need anything and then back home to tidy up the kitchen and do the beds, etc. I usually stop around 10.30–11.00 because I feel a bit tired, so I'll sit and have a cup of tea and more biscuits. Again, I do the 'I'll only have two', but have more. After this I tend to meet up with friends for an hour or so. I used to like to play tennis but I feel self-conscious. I sometimes go swimming or to aqua aerobics, but as time has gone by I feel less motivated, especially as some of my friends are really slim – I feel like a real lump next to them. We often eat lunch out – they like salads and things like that. I reluctantly follow suit, unless I'm with someone who will eat something 'naughty', and then I'll happily have chips. As I've said before, I do get tired and feel the need for something to pep me up.

Then it's time to get the kids from school. I pick them up and we're home for 4-ish. They like a drink and a snack and I tend again to have something to nibble. I get supper ready for John, who gets home at about 6.30. I like to do a proper meal with meat or fish and vegetables or maybe pasta, something filling. After we've eaten I'm clearing up, getting the children to bed, getting stuff ready for in the morning. I tend not to sit down until about 9.00–9.30, depending on what's on TV, then I like a glass of wine and some peanuts, chocolate, crisps – something like that, just as a treat.

One thing that stands out from 'a day in the life of Louise' is that she has some habits with food that will have to change for the weight to stay off. She also seems to be using food because she gets tired or needs a boost, so she is going for a lot of sugary or carbohydrate-laden foods. Unfortunately this causes her blood-sugar levels to go up and down quite dramatically, which will ultimately cause her to feel tired. In this respect she is caught up in a vicious cycle that needs to change. She is, by her own description, a 'nibbler' and needs to stop that – she is like many women with young children who fall into the trap of eating their leftovers or joining in on snacks that she could probably manage without. In the evening it is interesting that her treat is the wine and either nuts, chocolate or crisps. So, like lots of people, she also uses food as a treat.

The exercise is useful information for Louise in terms of her goal. It provides her with the facts of the matter, and demonstrates in no uncertain terms what has to be different this time. This is quite a harsh reality, as it provides no quick fix but, sadly, there usually aren't any.

Louise has also shown that she is an organized and well-motivated person. She deals with her children and her home very well. She prepares in advance and is certainly not afraid of hard work. She does, however, need to change her habits once and for all.

With this information she can add some clauses to her goal of wanting to lose weight. She can now add 'keeping it off' by:

1 Not eating biscuits before breakfast, but perhaps eating one of her two slices of toast at this time.
2 Not eating the children's leftovers. (She could tell herself she's not the dustbin!)
3 Not eating biscuits at elevenses but a piece of fruit instead.
4 Thinking more about what she needs at lunchtime. If she cuts down on sugar and carbohydrate she will probably feel less tired anyway.
5 Starting to play tennis and do other exercise again. Not only will she be enjoying herself, but she will also be getting fitter, which will, again, help her with the tiredness.
6 Not having afternoon tea with the children. Does she actually need it, or is it a habit?
7 Thinking about having a glass of wine without a snack.

Many of these points are simply about changing habits. Louise did not always eat like this – it is something that has developed over time. She *can* make those changes so that she can reach her goal weight and, most important of all, she can maintain it and start feeling really good about herself again. This also came out in the inventory – she feels self-conscious and compares herself to her slim friends.

Finally, Louise has also added a challenge to herself in terms of how she 'sees things'. She recognizes that she tends to dwell on everything that she needs to do and tends to make herself feel very overwhelmed and tired as a result. She has also decided to make a point of working on this as a way of helping her move towards her main goal. She can see that weariness and feeling overwhelmed certainly drive her to the biscuit tin!

Simon's goal is to change jobs, so in his 'day in the life' he was asked to concentrate on his working day, from which some very interesting things come to light.

Simon

My name is Simon and I'm 32 years old. I recently got divorced and have no children. I hate my job and have hated it for years. I work in the IT department of a large company. I sort of ended up working there by mistake. I didn't have any particular ambition when I left school and really didn't know what to do. This is my problem – I want to change my job, but I don't know what I really want to do.

Simon is a very 'visual person' (look back at Chapter 3 pages 50–53 if you need to remind yourself about this), i.e., he thinks in pictures. If he is thinking about something it can be either like a photograph or a video or film playing, so it can have movement and sound. When Simon thinks about leaving or wanting to change his job his mind goes blank – there is no image and he can't think what he wants to do. We ask Simon to concentrate on his 'day in the life' and not to get stuck on trying to come up with his goal.

Well, I get up about 7.30. I have to leave the house by 7.50, so I don't bother to eat – I just wash quickly and shave, throw on my clothes and get out. I tend to stop off at a sandwich bar or café and buy a coffee and a danish pastry on the way. I get to work on time by the skin of my teeth. Actually, a lot of times I'm late and I get filthy looks from people. I work as part of a team, which I don't always like and I know that they feel I let them down with my attitude. Not that I'm bad at my job, but I just don't particularly like the corporate life. We are expected to do lots of 'team-building' stuff – we have 'away days' and go off for weekends on trips. I just feel rebellious – I don't like being forced into the team or to be made to feel that I belong to the company. It's silly, but I just don't like it.

Anyway, where was I? I've got lost on my hate list rather than telling you about my day. Well, actually, I don't know what to say about my day. I start at 9.00 (if I get there on time). We tend to have a team meeting at 9.15 and then I start work at 10.00. When I get going I'm fine. I'm great if I am just left to my own devices. Sometimes I can have a piece of work and I am left to it – that is when I'm at my best – but most times I'm having to deal with loads of other people and their ideas and petty politics. That really does drive me mad. When I'm just ploughing through stuff I'm fine. I am considered very good at what I do, which is probably why I get away with my rather maverick behaviour.

I break for lunch at around 1.00. I tend to go off to the local pub and get a good lunch and sneak a couple of halves (beer). I shouldn't, because I know it's disapproved of, but I don't get drunk or anything like that. Then it's back to work. I just try to keep my head down and I work through until about 7.00. I'm divorced, so I live on my own. I tend to go off to a pub near my flat and get a meal and have 2–3 pints of beer. I don't drink a lot, but it just helps me wind down and it's an opportunity to set the world to rights with a few guys who drink there regularly. I tend to go home about 9.30–10.00 – I watch television and go to bed about 1.00.

This exercise helps Simon work on his goal in a way that he didn't expect. Through doing his day in the life he discovers that it is the environment that does not work for him, not the job itself. In fact, he says that he knows that he is good at what he does and is fine providing he can work on his own as much as possible. These issues have clarified what the problem is with his work: before doing the exercise he tended to go round and round in circles lumping all the unhappiness into one basket and saying that he hated his job, needed to leave and just didn't know what to do instead. Now that he has done this exercise he, at long last, feels motivated to move forwards. His goal is clear and specific – he needs to work in a small organization or one that does not have that corporate philosophy. He also needs to work in a place where he can take ownership of projects. He is willing to work in a team, but prefers to work on his own.

Simon also needs to make some changes to ensure that he can achieve the goal of finding a new job and keeping it. Living alone for the first time in six years after his divorce, he is not looking after himself properly.

> Oh, you want me to talk about how I'm feeling about being on my own. The divorce was not a bitter one. We both realized that we weren't right for each other. I'm still, obviously, very sad, but I am really finding it hard to adjust. That's why I don't spend any time in the flat. I have hardly any furniture. I have hardly anything that makes the flat look like a home. I hate that. It is also a complete pigsty and I don't want to cook and I just about get my washing together to get it laundered. I'm eating rubbish, drinking too much, and generally feeling very out of sorts.

We talked to Simon about how he needs to get 'his house in order' – literally. He needs to make his home a home, and start living there properly and taking better care of himself. If you think back to the end of Chapter 4 and the whole-person concept (pages 78–82), you will see how Simon is not looking after himself in any sense – physically, mentally, spiritually, socially or emotionally. Neglecting himself will not bring any positive outcome. Perhaps he needs to get himself in order before he completely decides upon his goal, as for some people there is a risk that they are simply changing something in the hope that they will feel better.

■ Making a thorough inventory

Now you have read two very different case histories. Louise is happy in most areas of her life. She sees her weight issue as something that is distinct and not a symptom of some deep-seated problems or problem areas in her life. Simon's desire to change his job needs closer examination. He definitely finds his work environment difficult, but being late, disorganized, not taking care of himself, and, presumably, arriving at work looking dishevelled would not be good things to take to a new job. We strongly suggested to him that he needed to make some fundamental changes to ensure his success in pursuing his goal. His skills are not in doubt, but could you imagine the scenario of him turning up for an interview late, in crumpled clothes and probably smelling of last night's lager?

■ Is your house in order?

Take your time to work on each section. Think hard about each question, because if you don't you may well miss out on something that will be a key issue in terms of your success or failure with your goal. This exercise also helps test and clarify your motivation – sometimes your motivation can be nothing less than unhelpful and potentially destructive, and we want you to be aware of this. To put it simply, don't set a goal to try and mend another area in your life. You may need to mend that area first, and then consider whether your goal is appropriate or not.

Write down your answers to each question to make the exercise easier to review. We've left space for you to be able to do this: see the following pages.

■ Home life

How is your home life in more practical terms? Ask yourself questions like:

Is my home life working for me?
Is it in any way a block to progress, or is it an area that I am comfortable with?

For example, Simon's lack of home life and lack of structure is a problem for him.

Are there current pressures at home that are creating problems for you? For example, it may be that you have a partner who is ill, or relationship problems, or children who are at a very challenging stage and there are lots of arguments at home.

It might be that you are under a lot of pressure because of your financial situation.

Do you struggle to make ends meet?

Do you feel resentful because you have to work so hard that you have no life at home?

Be aware of problems that may be motivating you, but motivating you falsely.

We are not suggesting that people have to have perfect families and perfect lives – that is not possible. What we do want you to do is to take stock of areas that are causing you serious difficulties – Simon's case history is a good example. Also, what you find stressful or potentially problematic is a truly personal issue, so don't compare yourself to other people, e.g., 'Oh, they cope so why can't I?' This type of self-talk is completely unhelpful. Also, don't look to change one area in your life to try and make you feel better about another one. Sometimes you need to challenge your goals and address what is really wrong.

■ Relationships

Think about your relationships. Ask yourself if are there serious problem areas and whether you see any of them as a potential block.

■ Social life

Do you have a social life? Some people really don't these days. Are you in contact with friends? Do you have trusted people that you can talk to and have a laugh with? Do you have hobbies or are you always working or looking after children and home?

■ Mental and emotional health

How are you mentally and emotionally? This is a serious question and we would urge any of you who have fears around your mental (or physical) health to consult a doctor. A book like this will not give you answers to serious conditions. What we can do, though, is encourage you to get help and understand that there is no shame in admitting that something is wrong. It can be one of the best things that you can do.

Questions you need to ask yourself are:

Do I suffer from very low moods, poor sleep, a change in appetite, a bleak feeling when I wake up in the morning and a lack of energy? These can be symptoms of depression and if you are experiencing such feelings you should consult your doctor.

Am I drinking too much? Your drinking pattern may have changed or you might be drinking more than you normally would. Again, if you are very worried this book cannot give you answers, but don't have your goal ruined because you are going through difficulties with alcohol.

Am I abusing drugs? Is my use of drugs getting in the way of relationships or work?

Am I held back by great feelings of anxiety and panic? Panic attacks are often characterized by feelings of loss of control and, sometimes, fearing that you might die from panic.

Do I battle with a lower grade of anxiety and panic and would like to learn strategies to overcome these feelings?

■ Work skills

If you are working, how would you describe your skills? June, a 40-year-old secretary, says her skills are: 'organization, good communication with clients and good keyboard skills'.

How would you describe your grey areas? Sarah is a trainee accountant. She tell us, 'I am disorganized and lack motivation.'

At work, what do you like doing?

You are not obliged to do something simply because you are good at it. A lot of people feel that they have a duty to do something because they are good at it, or that they should enjoy doing something because they are good at it. Later on in life, in particular, people can feel that they want to stop doing something because they are bored with it or because it no longer brings any sense of achievement. Achieving and being fulfilled are very important aspects of our journey through life.

You might also want to consider making an appointment with a consultancy that specializes in exploring your strengths and weaknesses in terms of your job. These sessions are not cheap, but they can provide you with a wealth of valuable information.

■ Other skills

Not all of you will be working. Some of you may see skills exhibited through other experiences and parts of your life. Think about what you are good at. Are you a good parent? Are you a good communicator? Are you organized in general? Also think about the things that you are not good at – Simon from our case history, for example, sees himself as a poor homemaker.

Achievements

Do you feel reasonably fulfilled? Or are you frustrated and feeling a lack of achievement in your life?

▓ Principles, values and beliefs

It is important to think about your principles. Principles are your standards and rules in terms of personal conduct. These will impact upon your goals. Remember that your goals need to be in accordance with your principles, otherwise you are going to be in difficulty. For example, a very competitive environment may not suit you if you feel that you have to capitalize upon other people's shortcomings or failures.

Consider, too, what your values are. These are your moral principles and beliefs.

Finally, what is your belief system? What are your opinions and convictions, the things you accept as true? Beliefs are often linked with religion, but obviously also encompass other important areas in your life.

Think about these aspects and areas of your life and write your findings down.

▣ Needs

Your needs are fundamental and therefore cannot be ignored or escaped. We perhaps rank them differently but they exist for all of us.

1 Physiological needs. These include:

food

drink

shelter

escape from pain

sex

2 Psychological and emotional needs. These include:

safety

attachment and love

esteem

self-actualization (fulfilling one's potential)

Remember that to meet your needs you must first recognize them. Look at this list and think also about how you currently rank your needs. Be aware that there is often a 'tug of war' between the two most powerful needs that you have – relationships and achievements. Jack, for example, declined a promotion because it meant spending more time away from home, and he knew that with two young children his wife would find it incredibly hard not having him around. Do think about this 'tug of war': it can help you be aware of potential conflicts in terms of your needs and the goals that you may be considering. It will help prevent you starting upon a goal and getting wrong-footed along the way. Don't take conflicts as a reason not to proceed: you need to respect the conflicts, discuss them with the people in your life and see if there is a way forward.

▣ Me, myself, I

This has started you thinking about your strengths, the areas that you need to work on, or be aware of as possible blocks, and things that really interest and motivate you. You have looked at your lifestyle, your commitments and how best to balance these against the way you set about achieving your goal. As we have said, many people have a conflict between two of their needs: the need to achieve and the need for relationships. You might find that there is very little conflict, or there may be a lot to balance, and if this is the case we will help you more in the planning stage – Chapters 7 and 8 – with this. Doing your personal inventory will have also helped you to begin to think about your priorities (not anyone else's). Remember that this is about *your* goals, and not other people's expectations of you or someone else's unfulfilled dream. You must dream your own dream, no matter how great or small.

This might be a good moment to read back over your personal inventory, and perhaps go over again some of the things you've learned about yourself. You might like to summarize your personal inventory here. Don't forget, this isn't necessarily fixed. You might return to this in a few months' or even years' time and realize just how far you've come.

If you want something different, you have to do something different

Chapter 6
Believing in and empowering yourself

❏ Give yourself permission

❏ Psyche yourself up

❏ Understand your 'drivers'

Each one of you reading this book will have picked it up to pursue a different goal. You might be developing skills such as computer literacy, or you may be tackling a problem area in your life. Whatever your goal is, think a lot more about yourself, what you can build upon and what you could be capable of. Keep your focus and it will help you stay on track. This chapter is all about building yourself up.

▓ Taking care of yourself

Think of your personal inventory as a prompt for an MOT. If you are physically below par, then why not consider what you are willing to do to improve that. Don't worry, we are not setting you goals to add to the ones you already have, it's just that you can do lots of things to improve your chances of success. That doesn't mean that you have to take up jogging, but you could make small improvements, such as walking three times a week for ten minutes, or using the stairs at work. Remember that every little bit counts.

Likewise, if your inventory has shown that there are medical issues that you are worried about, why not go for that check-up or doctor's appointment – you don't need to be held back from achieving your goals because you are preoccupied with your health. That is a key issue: sometimes people who are capable of achieving their goals don't make it because something has got in the way that really needn't have.

▓ Treat yourself as if you are worth it

This leads on to something else which is important. We want you not only to think about what you need to do to believe in yourself, we also want you to start behaving as if you are worthwhile, which means looking after yourself. Treating yourself as if you are valuable is an ingredient of being successful. On occasion, not looking after ourselves can cause conflicts with goals:

1 I have always wanted to learn to play tennis but I'm too fat.
2 I have always wanted to go to college but my life of clubbing and partying means that I never get my act together.
3 I always wanted to go back to work when my children reached five,

but I have been having panic attacks for a few years and I can't think of working until I sort myself out.

4 I have always wanted to work with people, but I feel self-conscious because I have bad teeth.

We are sure that you will see how certain areas in your life can create blocks to moving on with a goal, or become the excuse not to go for it. Sometimes empowering yourself and believing in yourself will involve tackling areas that you don't feel good about. Improving your health, for example, increases your self-esteem and confidence, all of which makes for a solid foundation when you are working on your particular goal.

Blueprints for success

Let's now really focus on what empowering yourself means and how you can start to 'believe in yourself'. We are always very interested in what we call 'blueprints for success'. These can be found from lots of different sources. Sometimes our parents can provide an excellent blueprint, but in our rapidly changing world that is often not the case. Many of us end up being very different from the backgrounds we grew up in and, in our work as therapists, people often say, 'I wish I had a parent who understood my life so that I could go to them for advice or guidance.' In other cases, when a parent could provide useful support, people prefer not to go to them.

A useful blueprint could come from someone else you know or admire: either someone you know personally and can speak to, or a person you've read about or heard interviewed. Always make an effort to pay attention to people that you consider have achieved their goals – you can learn from them. Listen to their tools and strategies.

Negative blueprints

Perhaps you come from a family that gives some strong negative messages about achieving goals and you may well have written about some of those in the gremlin exercise on page 67. In fact, you may have been exposed to a 'blueprint' that teaches you that something is not worth trying because it won't happen. Not only will you have to work hard at silencing some pretty strong messages, you also will have to work hard at finding more positive blueprints from people you know or admire. We are sure that you have all heard interviews on chat shows with very successful people who recall their school reports stating that they will 'come to nothing'. Despite such negative messages these people have succeeded against all predictions. As we have said earlier, a big part of achieving a goal is to 'see it, feel it, hear it and imagine it', and a big part of generating and maintaining motivation is to 'believe it' – to silence self-doubt and negative messages, and adopt the 'can do' frame of mind.

Let us take you through some negative messages that people give themselves when they are contemplating a goal:

1 What's the point? I'll never do it.
2 I always fail.
3 People like me don't achieve.
4 I'm afraid of failing.
5 I lose my focus every time – I've done well before and then slipped back.

We are sure that you will have written some very similar messages when you did the gremlin exercise and that you can add many negative messages to our small list. We are also sure that you can see some themes in these messages.

1 *'I'll never do it.'* How interesting that you can picture the future with the goal not being achieved. Now you have read Chapter 3 the danger of this thinking will make greater sense to you. As you now know, not only do you have to think about your goal, you need to step into the video of you doing it and feel the feelings. As you have learned, this is a very different experience from that of someone who has an idea and then promptly tells themselves not to bother.

2 *'I always fail.'* John, for example, always says this. When he does, his whole demeanour changes: his shoulders slump and the tone of his voice becomes monotonous. He looks like a failure when he says it. We challenge him on it: does 'always' mean that he has never succeeded at anything? We confront him until he admits that this simply is not true. Yes, he has had some failures, but he admits that the use of the word 'failure' is a bit of a sweeping generalization. As

he talks about one specific example of starting a new business it actually sounds as if there was some success, and as he talks he sits up and his shoulders rise. His problem came around 11 September 2001 when his source of capital dried up. It was extremely depressing and upsetting, but it was not his fault – it was sheer bad luck. He had given himself another negative message, which was very understandable, 'I'm just not lucky.' He had done what a lot of people do – he believed that one very bad experience had marked his card forever. So, again, we challenged him: we asked him to do the inventory exercise in the previous chapter and look at the fact that there were successes in his life. John needs to start speaking to himself as if he were successful

3 *'People like me don't achieve.'* This is a dangerous one, but if you look at successful people or people that have had dreams and achieved them, they come from all walks of life and are very different and diverse people. There is no one characteristic uniting them. People like you *do* achieve.

4 *'I'm afraid of failing.'* This is something that holds a lot of people back. We also think that fear gets more powerful as we get older. Have you ever noticed how children will often just have a go at anything and will see the funny side when something goes wrong? When we are older we can be frozen by fear. Remember that fear stands for False Evidence Appearing Real. We imagine the worst – we picture it and feel the feelings, even when it hasn't happened. You also need to watch the word 'failure': things can go wrong, but they don't have to be seen as failures – instead they can teach you what needs to be done differently.

5 *'I slip back.'* This is a big one. A lot of you reading this book will identify with this, and it is a dangerous reference point. 'Yes, I can do x for a while, but then I slip back.' Dieting is a good example to illustrate this point. People start diets. They might, for example, commit to eating a certain number of calories per day and make an agreement that they will not eat certain food such as chocolate. They keep going for two weeks and then decide to have some chocolate to reward themselves. Then the rot sets in, other foods are reintroduced, the calories are no longer counted or the 'bad foods' are ignored in the calorie count, and eventually the whole thing unravels. Remember, if you keep doing what you do you will simply get more of what you already have. Let's translate that into plain English. You are either on a diet or not. If you have committed to a diet and made a plan, which we talk about in Chapter 8, then your only reason for failure is that you have stopped following your plan.

Let's look even more closely at this example. Emma has been gaining weight over a period of two years. She is not particularly careful what she eats when it comes to her meals, but her real downfall is chocolate and biscuits. Her plan specified that she would reduce to 1500 calories a day and that would entail her eating a low-fat diet. She also decided that she would avoid chocolate and biscuits because she is never able to have 'just one' – she knows that her self-control is bad. So, her plan unravels because she tries to do something that's impossible for her – eat just a little chocolate. She is better off sticking to no chocolate no matter how hard that is at the beginning, because then she is not trying to control the uncontrollable.

So, a more honest representation of statement number 5 would not be: 'I do well for a couple of weeks and then I slip back,' but would be the more honest: 'I'm fine when I stick to my plan – the trouble starts when I try to do something that I know I can't do! I need to stick to my plan and be honest about what will sabotage it.' Thinking this way would actually get Emma believing in herself.

▓ Use positive self-talk and 'keep it in the day'

Now that you've read this far in the book we hope we've got you talking more positively to yourself. Positive self-talk promotes that 'can do' frame of mind.

Let's go back to the example of Emma with her diet. She is now more honest about where previous diets have gone wrong and she is on the path of taking responsibility and realizing that success is about not deviating from her plan. She made the plan for a reason and it would be ridiculous (but very human) not to follow it. She is now not in the 'failure' frame of mind, or the 'it is just a matter of time before I slip back' frame of mind. She now, therefore, needs to start some positive self-talk. If you're at a similar stage to Emma in working towards your goal, now is a good time to try this, too. Start saying things like, 'I can do it.'

Here's a useful device: 'keep it in the day'. Concentrate as much as you can on the day you have ahead of you. When you are working on a goal you might have to think somewhat about the future, but the more you can 'keep it in the day' the better, particularly if you are struggling. Again, using positive self-talk you can say things like, 'I just need to concentrate on today – so far I am sticking to my plan and that's good.' If doubts set in, you need not only to confront the negative but bash it with a positive, e.g., counter 'I'm going to fail' with 'What's more, I'm going to succeed,' or, 'This time is going to be different because I'm going to make it different.'

Getting yourself psyched up

Think about the haka (the chanting that the New Zealand All Blacks rugby team does before playing) and get yourself psyched up by telling yourself things like:

I can do it.
I'm going to do it.
Nothing is going to stop me.
I deserve this.
I can change and I'm going to.

Keep that head of yours busy with positive and motivating statements rather than those old negative statements.

The four permissions

Another key to achieving any goal is to be willing to accept that it is okay not to know things – what is much more important and much more useful is to be willing to learn and not to be put off easily. This obviously particularly applies when you wish to build a skill or learn something new. People can feel afraid of learning because they're frightened they will make a fool of themselves, or they are somehow ashamed of needing to learn whatever-it-is and not knowing it already. When adopting a 'can do' frame of mind you need to be willing to speak to yourself in tones that encourage and you need to give yourself the key permissions.

The key permissions you should give yourself are these:

Give yourself permission not to know.

Give yourself permission to learn.

Give yourself permission to make mistakes.

Give yourself permission not to have to be the best.

■ Understanding your drivers

The final piece of the jigsaw puzzle of 'empowering yourself' and 'believing in yourself' is for you to learn about and understand your 'drivers', i.e., knowing and understanding what 'drives' you or motivates you. Your drivers can be powerful positive forces that must be understood and harnessed to make them work effectively and productively. If not, they can hinder you, disempower you, and propel you backwards.

Drivers can motivate you or derail you. Another way to describe them is that they are powerful internal forces that either work for you or against you when trying to achieve goals. As there are many types of drivers, you need to learn to recognize the ones that can be used positively and to be aware of those that will have a negative effect.

We created the idea of 'drivers' when talking about Beechy's battle with addiction which, happily, ended over 20 years ago. We were talking about the times when he was so self-destructive, and it became very clear that he was 'driven' in one direction only and that was towards destruction and negativity. He would sabotage every good thing that anybody tried to do for him. He would turn everything around to the negative. Consequently, all he ever got was negativity. Now, some people might think that the reason he behaved like that was because of the alcohol and drugs he was taking at the time. But the reality was that the behaviour was more about him than the substances he was using. With or without the substances, this tendency, or 'driver', existed. So, today, he still has to be very careful. Just because he is not using alcohol or taking drugs doesn't mean to say that he won't behave in a negative or destructive pattern.

At all times, he has to take responsibility for the way he behaves and for the way he drives himself. Understanding yourself and understanding your drivers empowers you.

■ Take responsibility

In empowering yourself you need to take responsibility in every sense of the word. If you have become trapped in the 'failure script', telling yourself 'I always fail', not only do you have to confront the veracity of the statement by asking 'always?', you also need to look at your part in something not working out – take responsibility. Look back at the example of Emma and her diet. It didn't go wrong by magic – it went wrong because she made a conscious decision not to do what she knew she needed to do. She stopped taking responsibility and was not honest with herself. Be master/mistress of your destiny – it is in your hands to an extent, and you need to take ownership of it. You can make a positive step towards your goal today, or you can go in the opposite direction – the choice really is yours. Get powerful. Believe in yourself.

■ Don't be held back

Watch out for what we call 'safety drivers' – these are the drivers that don't let you take risks. They convince you to stay with the familiar and that change will be uncomfortable and difficult. These drivers convince you to think about all the things that can go wrong, and start to fill your screen with those images and the feelings they bring up. Having said that, we are not suggesting that you don't think goals and consequences through, but the issue is to give the positive and the negative an equal airing and see how they balance out. Also you need to understand which negatives are FEARs (False Evidence Appearing Real) as opposed to tangible negatives. Remember this saying:

> *Keep doing what you are doing and you are going to keep getting more of the same.*
> *If you want something different, you are going to have to do something different.*

■ Drivers

Here is a list of some drivers to help you start looking at your own. Really look at the list and be very honest with yourself about what drives you. This exercise should also alert you to the way we can sometimes pursue goals because we think we should, rather than because they really are our goals. Good examples of drivers that some people don't like to own up to are financial drivers, power drivers and status drivers. There is, of course, nothing wrong with these drivers, but you do hear people say, 'I don't like to admit that I'm very driven by money.'

Can you spot any of your drivers amongst these? We will continue to add to this list as we work on in the book – we could never print them all out, and we are sure you can add your own to the list:

Fear
Anger
Loneliness
Love
Trust
Excitement
Spirituality
Status
Image
Pride
Self-esteem
Money
Power
Authority
Competition
Defensiveness
Relationships
Sex
Work
Duty
Satisfaction
Affirmation
Needs (see page 106)

What do you think your drivers are? Write them down. You can always cross something out again if you realize that it isn't the driver you thought it was, that it was perhaps hiding something else. (What was it hiding?)

▉ Using your drivers

Once you start spotting your drivers you can start to become more aware of what motivates you, and this can act as a gauge to measure the appropriateness of what you are thinking of doing.

Spotting your driver is partly an intuitive thing. It can help if you 'picture' what you are thinking. Let's take the example of having a task to do as your goal. How many times do you get into the frame of mind that you can't or won't do it? The chances are that you would not have really thought of tackling it in the first place. How many times do you go to start something and then talk yourself out of it? If you manage to convince yourself that you can't do it you will be left feeling very inadequate. Not only that, you will also be very angry because you know, deep down, that you can do it. Most times, tasks aren't completed because of a fear that seizes you and tells you that you can't do it, or that it won't be very good, or that you will fail. Remember, though, that good feelings come from the completion of a task. So again, if you break the task down into stages, you will have the opportunities along the way to affirm yourself (which is a great driver). Also, think about how easy it is not to do something if you don't make a tangible commitment. If you make this type of commitment, then you will allow some powerful drivers to kick in, such as obligation, duty, excitement, success, etc.

Let's recap on the process of using your drivers effectively:

1 Identify the goal
2 If you start to think about what could go wrong, ask yourself what negative drivers are in play.
3 Challenge the negative thinking and get in contact with your positive drivers, such as 'excitement' and 'achievement'.
4 Make a commitment – this will wake up several potential drivers such as 'obligation', 'duty', 'competition' and' fear of failure' (which can be used positively).
5 Break the task down into stages so that you can drive yourself on each time you have completed another portion. This will help access your 'confidence', 'self-esteem', and 'satisfaction' drivers.

Make some notes here.

■ Confronting negative drivers

You need to decide right now that you are going to stop letting negative drivers get in your way. Put the book down for a moment and think about your most recent examples of setting a goal for yourself and not achieving it. In this way you can look at the history of your negative self-talk. Why not start to get annoyed about this thief – this behaviour or habit that steals opportunities from you?

Doing this should help you quickly to build a picture of what has been happening. By confronting these drivers and recognizing their negative effect, you will be getting out of the way of yourself. Also, don't be seduced by thinking that it is okay to have some sort of 'protective driver' when that protective driver does nothing but get in the way of you trying out a plan or new idea. Don't be the one who stops you from doing the things that you want to do – why shouldn't you do them? Take a risk. In fact, start taking some big risks. Listen to the story of any successful person and you will hear that they took risks to achieve.

Keep fighting the FEAR driver. Think about a time in your life when you have had to do something that you were afraid of and you did it well. You will remember, if you get really specific and imagine yourself back in that scenario, all the different negative images you conjured up. As you continued to build the pictures you will have been filling yourself with false evidence. Despite this false evidence, your experience was a success. Yes, you may reflect on past occasions when things have gone wrong, but there is nothing to suggest that history has to repeat itself. You can decide to picture something positive – that would be as 'real' as picturing something negative. You are not a clairvoyant, so you really cannot predict the future, but you can choose to fill yourself with some positives. Believe in yourself. Start feeling the power of believing that this time you really can achieve your goal.

Access good feelings

Chapter 7
Planning, planning, planning: part one

❏ Get in the mood

❏ Choose your environment

❏ Use outside stimuli, such as films, music and scents, to

inspire and empower

As you know, the golden rule of real estate is location, location, location, i.e., the bedrock of a good property is where it is situated. This is something that cannot be changed and determines so much about the value of a structure that is built on it. Similarly, you can have the most brilliant goal in the world and it can be entirely possible to achieve, but if you don't do the groundwork then you can devalue and jeopardize it. You cannot ever over-plan, as long as you don't use planning as an excuse not to move forwards and get into the implementation and action stage. You can also use your planning time in order to consider obstacles, so that you can be prepared and ready to deal with them. You should also review some of the previous chapters and be alert to the mental blocks that mean you end up sabotaging yourself.

Before you start planning, we want you to remind you of some of the tactics already covered in the book so that you are in that 'can do' frame of mind. Just as an athlete trains to get ready for that big day, we have suggested that you consider your level of fitness mentally, physically, emotionally and spiritually. You need, as we have said, to be in the right frame of mind and be sufficiently fit to project success, strength and ability to perform whatever tasks are necessary to achieve your goal. The more competent you feel, that more competent your performance of your goal will be. The success of your goal will be a reflection of the way your image projects success – or not.

So let's just remind you of some of our strategies, acronyms and other information:

1 **F E A R – False Evidence Appearing Real** – don't get held back by fear. It can, in some ways, be like a 'guardian angel', but it can also stop us from ever moving forward. You have to use your judgement: we would never encourage you to do something foolhardy or, on the other hand, to live your life with a whole load of regret and missed opportunities waiting for you at the end of it.

2 **Self-limiting beliefs** – don't box yourself into such a tight corner that you set limits on yourself that shouldn't be there. Sometimes we really don't know our potential until we try, and it can take a lot of courage to adopt that attitude, but it can be so worth it. We so want you to grow into who you are rather than who you think you are.

3 S M A R T – be smart in every sense of the word. So be:

Specific

Measurable

Ambitious

Realistic

Timed

at all times while you are working on your goal. It's a great word and it's a great acronym.

4 Look at your **personal inventory** and remind yourself of your strengths.

5 Use mantras or **positive self-talk:**

I am going to do this.

I am going to succeed.

I deserve this.

I am good enough.

Nothing is going to stop me.

6 Use the **visualization** technique, taking the time to see yourself succeeding with your goal. Remember that we cannot move towards something we don't see. Think about the expressions people use when they are feeling hopeless or that they won't succeed: 'You know, I just can't see it.' 'I just can't see myself doing that.' 'In my mind's eye I just cannot imagine that.' You need to be able to do the opposite of this by using the exercise in Chapter 3 (pages 52–53).

7 **Tipping the balance:** this exercise is about understanding the balance of decisions (look back at Chapter 3, pages 57–59) and how we need to 'tip' the balance in the right direction so that we can fire on all motivational engines. This exercise teaches you to pay attention to making the shift towards action and positiveness really happen and stay happening.

8 Learn your **Bill of Rights** – look back at Chapter 4, pages 68–69.

9 Gain greater **self-awareness** through doing exercises like the 'teaching

someone to be you for a day' on page 86 – this exercise can help you see your assets more clearly and help you see any difficulties that might get in the way of you achieving your goal.

10 Understand your **drivers** and utilize them to help create and maintain momentum.

11 **Confront yourself**. If you feel anxious or afraid ask: 'What is the worst thing that can happen?' With most goals the answer will be, 'Not succeeding' you need to be able to challenge that fear of failure, as it will hold you back. And do you know what? Most people don't succeed all the time – they might not broadcast it, but they probably don't.

▨ Getting in the mood

You will be more aware and have a clearer picture of your own mental blocks having read Chapter 4 but let's just remind you of them in brief: they are called 'anchors' and are the things that hold you back. They include the perfectionism anchor, the fear and anxiety anchor and the no-luck anchor – for more on these see pages 70–75.

By now you should be confronting these blocks and starting to work towards that 'can do' frame of mind that we keep talking to you about. You will be moving towards a more positive frame of mind and will be 'getting in the mood' for achieving your goal.

As we have said, being organized is very important, as is taking care that your surroundings are as conducive as possible to what you are doing. We can't all sit in mahogany-panelled offices to make our plans, but we can try to create the best environment possible to get 'in the mood'. Try to have somewhere tidy and pleasant in which to work on your goal. It must be a place where you can concentrate on your plan and start to get motivated. Sitting, for example, in the kitchen with a pile of washing next to you is just not going to work, neither is sitting with the family playing around you.

Let's have a look at some other ways of influencing the way you are feeling. These involve looking more closely at your environment, and using outside stimuli, such as music, film, aroma, light and heat. Some of you may be well aware of the benefits in terms of mood enhancement, but are simply not putting them to their full use. Remember that every little bit helps. Something that may seem trivial can be helpful in keeping you on track, so don't ignore it. Many things have the power to help keep us stimulated and upbeat, and utilizing them can be very life-enhancing.

Using music

Use music that makes you feel good. A lot of research has been done into the effects of music on people's moods. Most of us listen to music in one form or another, and we don't think that any of us need research to tell us what we already know – music can lift our spirits or make us feel sad or nostalgic, or it can help us relax and feel peaceful. It is incredibly powerful. There are a lot of classical pieces in particular that are very rousing and definitely impact positively upon those who listen.

If you like classical music and have a favourite piece that motivates and inspires you, use it when you are planning and thinking about your goal. It can help get you in 'the mood' and into that 'can do' frame of mind. If you don't like classical music we are sure you have a contemporary piece of music that makes you feel powerful, energized and unstoppable when you listen to it. You can also encourage an association between feeling good about your goal and a piece of music. On occasions when you feel less enthusiastic you can put on that piece of music and allow it to access all the positive feelings that you had the last time you listened to it. It is a bit like an emotional 'cash dispenser': you key in and out pop lots of good feelings. You need to devise lots of different ways to access good feelings associated with achieving your goal, as well as just simply learning to take time to luxuriate in some nice feelings – it's a bit like taking a nice warm bath, except that you are soaking in affirmations and good feelings!

Not only does music stimulate you emotionally, it also stimulates your imagination and creative feelings. Perhaps your goal involves you being creative or using your imagination, or perhaps you need to imagine the outcome simply because you are going to embark upon something new that you haven't really experienced before. Be willing to experiment with different pieces of music. Some might work well when you want to think, others can get you 'in the mood', and there may be a few that you want to play afterwards to mull over what you have been thinking about.

Also think about using music in the visualization techniques that we have been suggesting you start to do. As you well know by now visualization really does help increase and maintain your motivation and can also to help you focus. Why not, when you have perfected 'stepping into that screen' when doing your visualization, add your favourite piece of music to it and see what happens – you will really feel that you are starring in an epic! It could add the finishing touch to your visualization.

James found music a very powerful addition to his visualization. His example is a little different from some that we have given, and we will speak some more about this technique later on in the chapter. This is what James does to get himself into a 'can-do' frame of mind, which is something quite separate from visualizing his goal.

To achieve my goal I will have to speak to a lot of people and will have to do presentations. I devised this visualization to get me in the mood to go and meet people to discuss my project, as well as having to do presentations to raise the capital. Please don't laugh; it is very *Boys' Own*.

I imagine myself as a knight on a huge black charger. There I am in the full metal outfit – the helmet with the visor, a breastplate and chain mail. The horse's face is covered by a visor and has various very ornate pieces of protective gear on its shoulders. I am entering a jousting competition and I am coming up against the most feared competitor. It is just like a scene in a film. I come into the arena and the crowd are there and they are shouting for me. They want me to win (I really try to get in contact with those feelings of someone rooting for me, a crowd shouting for me) I am completely unafraid because I am the up-and-coming knight – I've come from nowhere and am taking the world of jousting by storm.

The film I have borrowed this scene from used modern rock music and the song that played was 'We Will Rock You' by Queen. When it plays in the film all the crowd claps with the beat – it is very powerful and I often hear the song playing in my head and it immediately evokes the powerful feelings. I really do feel unstoppable.

This is an interesting example for several reasons. James is using a scene from a film, so he already has the powerful image – he just has to step into it. He has also connected with the music used in the film and the fact that the song was used to encourage the 'jouster'. This is an almost ready-made visual with music – and we will look at these next.

Let us make a few suggestions here of classical pieces you might like to listen to and see what they do for your mood.

Beethoven: Symphonies 1–9, Violin concertos, Piano sonatas
Bach: The French Suites, The English Suites
Handel: Oratorios, *Messiah*
Mozart: Symphonies, *The Magic Flute, The Marriage of Figaro*
Aaron Copland: *Fanfare for the Common Man*
Carl Orff: *Carmina Burana*
Holst: *The Planets*
Walton: *Belshazzar's Feast*
Verdi: Requiems
Duruflé: Requiems
Khachaturian: *Spartacus*

We spoke to John, who wants to get fit (see Chapter 2, pages 32–33 for more details of John's goal), about what he is doing to get himself in the mood. John will be working on making changes to his diet, drinking less alcohol, swimming once a week and playing football with his son at the weekend. Let's hear about his plan:

As 'getting fit' involves making changes in several areas, I have broken the goal down into those categories to think about planning. I have also decided to go upstairs to my bedroom (as it is quieter up there and I have cleared a small table where I have my computer so that I can sit and work on my goal and get prepared).

I love rock music and I do play some of my favourite tracks when I have finished my thinking time. It's funny, because if I hear any of those tracks inadvertently I now associate them with my fitness goal and how good I am going to feel, and I get a real surge of positive feelings.

■ Using ready-made visuals

You have already read a great example from James, but we cut it short because we wanted you to focus on how he used a particular song to make him feel good. So let's hear some more from him about 'borrowing' existing images to help motivate him:

> I chose the scene from this film because although it is actually a very light-hearted film, it just made me think about the goal that I want to achieve. No, I don't want to be a knight, but I saw the character as someone who has to prove himself in a world that at the beginning wouldn't recognize him – I suppose I thought the film was allegorical.
>
> I also liked the use of the contemporary music in the film and found the way they used the beat of the song almost like a chant from a football match. So I use this scene (obviously with me playing the part of the knight) to get me in the mood when I have meetings or am doing the presentations that I have to do to raise the money for my business project.

Think about films that have had a positive, motivating, energizing or powerful impact upon you. We are sure you have one or two you can think of. Write them down.

Lorraine uses the film *The Horse Whisperer*:

> I identify strongly with the film, not because I have ever been involved in a riding accident, but because I was very badly injured in a car accident. I use the scene when the girl gets on the horse for the first time as a very motivating scene for me. In fact, I first saw the film when I was injured and I felt very inspired by it and became determined to be 'that girl'. I use it to this day whenever I want to achieve something that feels hard or difficult. I just think of me stepping into that scene and I feel the feelings of fear and bewilderment melt into confidence and achievement.

Just as you can with music, you can also use films to stimulate. There are countless films that really are inspirational and motivating – some are perhaps more serious than others, but the end result is that they change the way you feel. Just stand outside a cinema when people are coming out and watch their moods: you will see by the looks on their faces what type of film they have seen.

▓ Using aromatherapy

Aromatherapy has deservedly taken its place as a credible and extremely beneficial therapy. The oils can be used in massage, or in burners, in the bath, or simply dropped onto a tissue and placed nearby the individual who wishes to benefit.

Smell is our first sense and also our most immediate sense. We are sure that all of you will have perfume-evoked memories that will feel incredibly strong. Interestingly, sight takes longer to be processed by the brain – aroma, by contrast, takes a more direct path to the brain and is almost instantaneously processed.

There are many wonderful books on this subject. For now, here are a few examples of essential oils you might like to use:

Relaxants:
Lavender
Ylang ylang
Rose Absolute

Jasmine
Frankincense
Sandalwood
Geranium

Energizers:
Lemon
Lemongrass
Mandarin orange
Peppermint
Orange blossom
Rosemary
Eucalyptus
Grapefruit

■ Your surroundings

Have you ever noticed in military films set in the eighteenth and nineteenth centuries how the generals who waged war are invariably depicted sitting in their tents with crisp linen and crystal glasses, etc.? These men obviously felt 'better' and perhaps felt more in control by having the trappings of their civilized world around them. We would imagine that they were also impressing upon those around them their superior rank. We don't necessarily need rich or sophisticated trappings, because not all of us can afford them, but we should try to surround ourselves with what makes us feel good and moves us into a work and success mode. Create a space that feels inviting.

'Inviting' is such a useful and powerful word – some spaces really are inviting and some are definitely not. Many of you will be very aware of the ancient Chinese art of feng shui, which promotes the creation of balance and harmony in living and working environments. Ask yourself if your space 'feels' good – am I happy to sit down and work here? Does this space make me feel motivated? One key way of making a space feel inviting would be to ensure that it is tidy and clutter-free. Not many of you will have a study or a spare room, but if you do, then exactly the same rules apply as to the rest of your living space. Spare rooms often tend to be dumping grounds for washing and things that don't have a place anywhere else, so if you work in a spare room, make sure that it's tidy and that what you are working on is organized and ready. Don't sit down and then spend an hour looking for something you can't find.

Lighting

Make sure that you have adequate lighting. This might seem a small thing, but makes a big contribution to your comfort. You might be lucky to have a window nearby, but otherwise get a good desk lamp, make sure that you make the best of your space and that you are as comfortable as possible.

We spoke to Clare about the environment she uses to plan and review her goal:

> I use a corner of my bedroom. I have put a table in front of the window and I have a smaller table next to it where I have a few books. The table has a couple of drawers, so I store my notebook and stationery in there and any-thing else that I might need. I am hopeless if I have to get up to look for something – I get easily distracted and also I don't have a lot of time, so I have to use every minute.

Clare's example pulls together several points about the best environment to have. She has some natural light and she sounds as if she has her space organized, tidy and clutter-free. She is also aware that she can use not finding something as an excuse to stop or be distracted.

With the environment ready, the next stage can begin.

No plan is a plan to fail

Chapter 8
Planning, planning, planning: part two

❏ Gather information

❏ Set micro-goals

We hope that you are now feeling 'in the mood' and in a 'can do' frame of mind. We also hope that you have had some fun with the previous chapter. It is important for you to enjoy your journey – working at something needs, on occasions, to be fun, and we certainly believe that in therapy people can make some incredible discoveries about themselves when they are unguarded and in 'fun mode'. When you are choosing the films for your 'ready-made' visuals, don't feel obliged to pick a serious film if a fun one will do. What's more, you don't have to share what you are doing with anyone else, so just go for it and enjoy …

Let's turn now to the steps involved in making a plan that will lead you towards achieving your goal. Remember above all that the first rule of success is that you must have a plan. In the business world you often hear the expression: 'No plan is a plan to fail.'

If you don't plan, then you are being very half-hearted about your goal and we'd wonder why you don't want to make the effort – what is stopping you or getting in your way? Perhaps you need to go back and re-read the chapter on 'blasting blocks' (Chapter 4) and put the planning exercise on hold until you are sufficiently motivated. Don't move forward with planning until you are in the right frame of mind. Remember what we said to you in Chapter 7: you must build a frame of mind that will assist you and keep you moving – striving towards a goal is something that you must put every ounce of effort into. You also shouldn't make a plan too elaborate – keep it simple and very clear.

Because everyone reading this book has very different goals, you must use the framework in this chapter as a guide. Certain parts will apply more to some people than others, but again the key thing is to plan and be organized. To help you we will show you different plans made by people who have worked with us, and you can pick out the steps that will make the framework work for you. What we do suggest for everyone is to give time to your plan – don't rush and don't oversimplify. The planning is the foundation for success.

▶ Here are the steps you need to go through when making a plan. Remember
▶ that you need to have set your goal as specifically as possible before
▶ embarking on your plan (have a look at Chapter 2 again, and at the notes
▶ you've made yourself there). You can move between the steps and can go
▶ back and forth as you work on your plan.

1 Information review

Re-read your personal inventory (see Chapter 5) and add anything necessary to your goal. This may be in the form of clarification, or identifying blocks.

2 Research and gather information about your goal

You may add to or amend your goal.

3 Set micro-goals (see this chapter)

4 Be SMART at all times (see page 32)

5 Be 'measured' and 'timed'

These two are particularly important when working on a goal. They are vital steps to ensure success, so you need to:

a Set targets – probably on a weekly basis. If things seem tough set targets on a daily basis

b Make time frames

c Make checklists

d Plot your progress

6 Build and maintain your motivation by using the above as a checklist

Remember that your plan is not only a to-do list – it also incorporates strategies to keep you focused and motivated. You need to attend to your levels of motivation as much as you need to attend to the micro-steps. Remember also to move back and forth between the steps as you plan – use new discoveries to create the clearest goal and the clearest steps to get there. Don't be put off by new pieces of information that might mean you have to re-think – use each discovery as a part of your path to success, not a cul-de-sac that ends in failure.

■ Attitude, attitude, attitude

We know that the goals of people reading this book are bound to vary hugely. Some of them will undoubtedly involve a lot of thought and planning, so you will need to do research and gather information for lots of different reasons. Some of you may be seeking nutritional advice because you want to lose weight; some may need details of courses or to find out what qualifications are needed for a particular job. Others who are considering starting a business will have a lot of research to do to determine its viability. Whether your goals involve steps that are simple and straightforward or very complex, treat your plan as an important task. Don't have a casual approach to it – see it as something that you need to attend to properly to give yourself the best possible chance. Also, be careful not to label a goal as easy or hard – look at it within the context of your life and your experience. A difficult goal for one person could be easy for another, and vice versa. Don't compare yourself unfavourably to others – by all means use them as a blueprint, but use others as a help, not a hindrance.

We will look at the steps of the plan in more detail later, but before we do that, let's look at how being specific about your goal can influence the planning. A good example is to look at Rebecca's goal – to lose weight – from Chapter 2. Just to refresh your memory, once Rebecca became more specific about her goal we suggested that this would impact upon the planning stage. Rather than the goal being simply about losing weight, it became: 'I want to lose 2 stones and thereafter I want to maintain my weight.'

So her goal became as much about maintaining weight loss as losing the weight in the first place. Rebecca had to be honest about what she does with food that causes her to re-gain the weight. To create an effective plan she needs to look at her eating patterns and relationship with food by doing the 'teach someone to be you for a day' exercise, which is first outlined on pages 86–87. She needs to be honest, specific and to make a firm commitment. If she changes nothing then nothing will change – all she will do is diet, then put the weight back on. She also needs to make sure that her knowledge about food, calories and healthy eating is accurate. She must build into her planning the changes she knows she needs to make – even if she does not like them! To achieve her goal she needs to consider permanent change, which should be reflected in her plan.

The first stage of planning after setting and re-defining your goal is infor-mation-gathering from your personal inventories and 'day in the life'. This involves gaining a greater sense of self-awareness as well as looking at informa-tion that can be particularly relevant to your goal. The information can also inform you and prepare you to deal more effectively with blocks and anchors.

To see this in action let's look back at Louise and the information she gathered from her day-in-the-life exercise (pages 87–90) and how this influences her final goal. As you read, Louise wants to lose weight because she wants to enjoy her tennis more and be able to dress differently. There is clearly an issue of self-esteem that losing weight would also address. Our concern is that she sees weight gain as a self-fulfilling prophecy, so to keep the weight off she has to start to confront what needs to change, rather than being a professional dieter all her life. Keep doing what you are doing and you simply get more of the same. Louise feels incredibly defeatist, which is completely the wrong mind-set to start working on a goal. If any of you recognize this feeling, then ask yourself: 'What changes do I need to make so that I can start believing that I can achieve my goal?'

Although you may not have any blinding flashes of self-discovery during your 'day in the life' exercise, you will certainly see your habits, patterns, thoughts and daily routine written down, probably for the first time. At worst, what you know about yourself will almost certainly take on a greater significance, and at best you will be seeing certain things about yourself in a different light. Most important of all is that the exercise helps prepare you to give your goal your best attempt – and also, there is no such thing as wasted knowledge. If you feel that you cannot be bothered to do the exercise, stop and ask yourself what is happening – why can't you be bothered to do something that will be very helpful? Also, do not fall into the trap of thinking. 'Why would this help?' If you were an expert on achieving goals you wouldn't be reading this book.

Re-read Louise's 'day in the life' and we will take you step by step through the way she uses the information to make her plan. Her goal was: 'To lose weight. To be specific, I want to lose 3 stones … My goal is also about admitting that I have to change my eating habits … to be honest I see my weight loss as something that is not permanent. I do think about the day I stop dieting and think about all the great things I'm going to eat!'

When Louise becomes more specific and more honest with herself, the goal becomes: to lose 3 stones and to change eating habits; to believe that weight loss can be permanent.

She has gone back and re-defined her goal further, so let's move on through your plan and Louise's, as we are using her as an illustration throughout this section.

■ Your plan

Step 1: Information review

Use the inventory, the 'day in the life', and the gremlin exercise to give you clarity and information about yourself. Re-read them and add anything necessary to your goal. Look back on the chapter on anchors (pages 70–75) and think about blocks – write them down again so that you can be more aware.

Let's look at the information Louise has gathered. Louise's 'day in the life' has clearly informed her about her eating habits and in part what drives them:

1 She definitely uses food to give her an energy lift – she is a busy mother and rushes around a lot. Because she wants that immediate lift she tends to go for high-carb and sugar-laden foods.
2 She tends to nibble and eats the children's leftovers.
3 As she has got fatter she has stopped exercising as much or tends not to enjoy exercise. She has also become more self-conscious and so she is caught in a very vicious circle.

Step 2: Research and gather information about your goal

In Step Three you will see what Louise does to start setting her micro-goals. Before she does this she needs to do some research by obtaining books on nutrition and looking on the internet. Many of you will need to do some type of research and this can be a real hurdle for a lot of people. Don't be afraid to admit that there are some things that you don't know – it is not a sign of weakness. In fact, it's the absolute opposite – being able to say 'I don't know' is a real sign of strength and wisdom. Likewise, there will be times when you may need to ask for help, which, again, is not a sign of weakness: we all need help from time to time, be it from someone who acts in a advisory capacity or a therapeutic capacity. Don't skimp on gathering information if you feel the time is very limited: you need to give your goal time to ensure success. Don't be daunted by the prospect of that or tell yourself that you can't or that you don't have time.

There are many sources you can use for research. Books are a good first step. If you want to change your eating habits then consider looking at books on nutrition. Don't pick up books that advocate faddy diets – they won't be helpful. You need objective facts, not facts that are geared towards selling a concept or product. Let's go back to Louise and hear what she has to say:

I certainly need to think about learning about calories and becoming more aware. I also don't want to do a faddy diet – I have tried them all and have found that I just go straight back to old habits. What I want to do is look at dieting on about 1500 calories a day. So I need to look at what I can realistically have: in the past I've just cheated and I have to stop doing that. It's pathetic, really, I know that I'm doing it, so I'm only cheating me. I will be looking at getting a calorie-counting book and I will also try and get a book on nutrition – I want to find out what people mean by a 'balanced diet'. I am also thinking of making an appointment with a nutritionist so that I can get some advice.

As you know we advocate the 'whole-person' approach in this book, so you know that we would encourage all of you to take better care of yourselves. Understanding more about food isn't only for those who specifically want to lose weight. Use the whole-person approach as an opportunity to make improvements in your life right across the board. You need to:

act like a winner and behave like a winner

There are numerous goals that can be furthered by doing some reading, and huge numbers of personal development books that you could turn to alongside this one. Just have a browse in your nearest bookshop or library.

To get information you could try:

Bookshops and libraries
Consultancies/agencies
The internet
People who have achieved goals themselves, whom you know personally
Universities and colleges that run relevant courses – you can always get a
    prospectus to give you ideas

Step 3: Break the goal down into micro-goals
Let's look at Louise again.

I have 3 stones to lose and I want to stop yo-yo dieting so I am going to have to approach this in a completely different way. Rather than focusing on how quickly I can lose weight, which means that I tend to eat in quite an abnormal way, I am going to focus on eating differently, on eating food that I know gives me a health kick. I am not going to focus so much on losing 3 stones – that is my end goal. I will focus more on changing my eating habits: I will write these down on a weekly basis and review them. I must be specific. My micro-goals for changing my eating habits are:

1 Stop eating biscuits before breakfast. If I need something I will have a slice of wholemeal toast.

2 Stop eating the children's leftovers.

3 No biscuits for 'elevenses'.

4 In fact, no biscuits at all – I never have just one or two. Unfortunately, I have to buy them for the children and my husband, but I am just going to have to get into the habit of not 'trying to control the uncontrollable'. I am almost like a biscuit addict.

5 Fewer carbohydrates at lunchtime. I am the Queen of Carbs, but I have read in lots of articles that they actually can make you very tired.

Remind yourself of your micro-goals.

Step 4: Be SMART at all times

You will notice that Louise is using the SMART skills that should be used throughout this exercise. She has been specific, she has set limits around quantities and timings, and is being realistic. If she – and anyone who is working towards achieving their goal – sticks to this, success is guaranteed. SMART skills generate and maintain motivation. Keep using them – they are the fuel that will drive you forwards.

Step 5: Be 'measured' and 'timed'

Set targets
Make time frames
Make checklists
Plot your progress

Step 6: Build and maintain your motivation by using the above as a checklist

Louise has written the following:

1 I have my target of my overall weight loss but I would like to commit to losing a minimum of 3 lb per week. I have tended in the past to want to lose weight very quickly, but that has led me into faddy dieting, rather than learning to change my eating habits.

2 If I calculate correctly, I am looking at a time frame of 14 weeks. I will write that date in the diary.

3 The checklist I am going to keep will be to keep a food diary. I will write down everything I eat, but more importantly, I am going to plan my food on a weekly basis and calculate the calories as a guideline. I will also put my exercise onto this chart so that I can take into account the calories I burn in addition to my daily requirement.

4 At the end of each week I will weigh myself. I am not going to fall into the trap of doing it every day, as that makes me very obsessive. If I have not hit the target then I know that I have to tighten up the next week. If I have lost more I won't change what I am doing, because I think that could lead to some bad habits.

5 In terms of motivating myself I certainly will use the checklists and give

myself a big pat on the back if I am achieving my targets. I also intend to motivate myself by the fact that I am taking responsibility – I am taking charge. I intend to 'stay the distance', which is something that I get very cross with myself about – I often feel that I bail out, but this time it will be different.

Now that you have seen one plan in action, let's show you another from start to finish.

Paul tells us:

> My goal is to start my own business. I am going to call it Handy Husbands, and it is to provide skilled tradesmen and handymen to households to work on small and large jobs. The key will be that I will have numbers of people on my books who will be personally known to me, so I can recommend their work and them as characters. I imagine that my services would be used a lot by women and I want the service to feel very 'woman-friendly'.

Or to be a bit more concise:

> My goal is to start a business that provides skilled tradesmen and handymen as a 'woman-friendly' service.

So, here is Paul's plan:

Step 1: Information review

When I did my work on my inventory and my 'a day in the life' and the gremlin exercise these were some of the key points that I want to carry forward and help me keep on track. The inventory work and the information-gathering about myself did not change my goal, but it did highlight a motivation problem and lack of confidence, which I need to put into my plan. I also realize that I am physically quite low and I know that working on that is going to make me feel better about myself. I will then look at my best when I go to the bank – I am sure that they aren't going to lend money to someone who looks tired and overweight and generally in a bit of a mess. It also brought home to me the influence of some very negative messages that I need to be wary of because they easily could get in my way.

Here are some other points I took from the inventory.

I have good skills, which give me confidence:
I am numerate, I am able to be organized, I have people skills

On the minus side:

- I am very unmotivated at the moment
- I am feeling lethargic and below par
- I eat and drink too much in the evening – it is all out of frustration
- I can lack confidence
- I know I will have to get a bank loan – so I need to be able to sell myself.

Let's look at the highlights from my 'day in the life': I usually wake at about 7.30. I have a wife, Susan and two children, Jack, four, and Aimee, two. I work in an accounts department of a large retail company and I have a drive of about 45 minutes to get to my desk for 9.00, so I tend to rush out in the morning. I am not at all enthusiastic about my job, which makes me bad at getting up and I tend to be very cranky with everyone. I tend to grab a quick breakfast of toast, throw on my clothes and go.

Paul then goes on to talk about his workday:

I feel very de-motivated at work. I work as part of a large team and feel that work is constantly being thrown at me and I don't get a chance to see something through from start to finish. I am not afraid of taking charge of a project and know that I work to a high standard and have good attention to detail. I also am fed up because I used to have a lot of client contact but now I don't – I do like dealing with people and feel that it is one of my qualities. My gremlin exercise was very good in terms of alerting me to blocks, which are:

1 I don't believe that people 'like me' are successful and start businesses.
2 My father used to say when he was angry, 'Who do you think you are?'
3 Other messages are: 'Don't take risks' and 'Careful you don't make a fool of yourself.'

Step 2: Research and gather information

I intend to go to some seminars on starting small businesses. I am also going to have an informal conversation with my bankers and find out what sort of loan they will give me. I will go through *Yellow Pages* and other resources to try to find how many people provide this type of service. I will ring a few of them to sound them out in terms of what they do and what they charge, as well as try to canvass people locally to see how they feel about this type of service and whether they would use it. I expect I will start with people I know and ask them if they would introduce me to someone else.

Step 3: Set micro-goals
Some of the goals come out of the research I will do as well as being the research:

1 Attend seminars.
2 Start working on my self-confidence and self-esteem by improving my appearance and improving my level of fitness.
3 Meet the bank informally.
4 Find out about a loan.
5 See what other similar services are in my area and 'phone around to see what they offer and what they charge.
6 Canvass some people locally and see how they feel about my service.
7 Start a dossier on tradesmen and handymen that I will use.
8 Start to write business plan.
9 Take the business plan to the bank to make a formal presentation.

Step 4: Be SMART at all times
I find that the SMART skills work very well in terms of keeping me on track and motivated. Because I am being specific about every task and every idea I have an opportunity to use that yardstick against which I can measure progress, so I find it very motivating. Most importantly, it makes me think before I act. Each time I have a new thought or idea I make myself get specific and it stops me from going off at tangents or doing something without thinking about how it will fit or how it will work. It has also helped me with being realistic – because everything is so much better thought through, I do go back and forth between the steps and hone everything. It has also changed my ideas about failure – I now see having to make changes if I come up against a brick wall as something that is probably inevitable and doesn't have to spell the end of my idea. As you saw from my gremlin exercise I am afraid of failure and looking stupid, so this has really helped me.

Step 5: Be 'measured' and 'timed'

These are my targets and timings:

1 My target each week will be to do one hour's work each evening after work and work for two hours each day over the weekend. If I do more that will be a bonus.

2 As I don't know how long each task will take, I would prefer to start like this and then I will fine-tune. Because I am committed to working these hours each week I feel that I will be moving things along and am not procrastinating.

3 I will set a deadline by making an appointment with my bank manager so that I have a date to work to.

4 Some of my micro-goals will make a good checklist, but I will try to break them down further.

5 I will look at my progress at the end of each week and perhaps set a target for the next week.

Step 6: Build and maintain motivation by using the above as a checklist

I will use the above to motivate me – I work well when I have a plan and do get great pleasure out of achieving what I have set out to achieve. As I said in step 4, I find the SMART techniques very helpful because they certainly keep me on track and because progress is measurable it creates motivation. I will always use these techniques whatever I am doing, because I have found them so beneficial – especially because I struggle to keep motivated.

You have now seen how truly useful planning is. As has been demonstrated through the examples given by Louise and Paul, if you follow the plan it really makes you think – and think in detail. What they have shared with us almost shows the internal conversations they have had with themselves, which we hope will encourage you to do the same. Paul's work on his inventory in particular made him aware of his blocks, fear of failure and lack of motivation. By using the plan effectively he has not only worked methodically, but he has also used the SMART skills in particular to keep him motivated. He also has shown that he has embraced the idea of the whole-person concept and he has shown 100 per cent that he wants to act, feel and look like a winner.

Continuity breeds success

Chapter 9
Affirming yourself

❑ You're on your way now

Affirming ourselves is not something that most people do habitually. We fall into patterns of living, and we just keep walking down the same old road that we've been walking most of our lives. All of a sudden, we've been asking you to walk down a new road. It's a very strange road, perhaps frightening, but very worthwhile. The key to staying on this road is by affirming yourself on a daily basis. This may seem a strange thing to do or to start doing but, believe me, it's going to pay off and it will make all your hard work seem very worthwhile. Nothing comes easy. Personal change is the hardest goal to achieve, so well done for getting this far.

■ What do we mean by affirming yourself?

Self-affirmation is a statement that comes from you. If you start to affirm yourself the chances of success in your goal will be high. For example, you could tell yourself that: you are going to achieve your goals; you are going to make some changes; you are going to work hard continually and not lapse back into your old behaviour. Self-affirmation is not something that you can dip in and out of – you need to do it on a daily basis, seven days a week. Even if you are not working on something consciously, you just need to tell yourself that you're worthwhile, that you're a good person and that you could be better, but you are doing your best. I know it will feel strange to start with, but it's something you can very quickly fall into the habit of.

Think back to the number of times you have told yourself: 'I can't do that: I wouldn't be good enough to do that,' or, 'There's no point in me even asking, they'll only reject me,' or, 'I wouldn't even think about doing that because I'd only fail.' All these messages are negative. And it's not rocket science that if you continually fill yourself up with negative messages, then all you will have is a negative outlook. What we're asking you to do is to reframe that. To change your way of thinking by telling yourself that you are worth it, that you can do it and that you are not going to fail. Affirmation is a commitment to you and you alone, and you are telling yourself that you are going to succeed. At the very minimum you can look at yourself in the mirror every morning when you get up and say, 'I am worth doing this for.' That would be better than half-a-dozen negative messages. If you want to take it a bit further and tell yourself that you're worth changing for and that you really want to do something about this situation in your life, then that will enhance your chances even more.

Self-affirmation is easy because it's so private and personal. No one else has to know about it: you don't have to go round your friends and say, 'I've just got to pop out for a moment to do some self-affirmation.' It's also a very useful tool when you are in a difficult situation, because you use your inner voice to say to yourself, 'I am not going to back down; I am not going to behave the way I would in the past. I am going to behave in this new way and I am going to stick to it no matter what.' This, believe it or not, will help you in difficult situations and in times of stress, when you feel that your back's against the wall and you've nowhere to turn. Self-affirmation can help you move forwards. Remember, it's all about you.

This is about your behaviour. It's about you telling yourself that you are going to achieve your goals and make some changes, and that you are worth changing for. Positive behaviour leads to positive change. You just have to do this one day at a time, no more, no less. Keeping everything in the day makes life so much easier, because we are so prone to projecting what we are going to be doing tomorrow, or in a couple of days' or next week or in six months. Life is not meant to be a struggle or a continual negative experience. Helping yourself to make things better will help to improve your quality of life. Remember, richness of spirit is the true wealth of life. In Chapter 4 we talked about the whole-person concept (pages 78–82), which involves the whole of you – physically, emotionally, mentally, socially and spiritually. If you continue to work on these parts of yourself, that will breed more and more success. Self-affirmation comes right alongside this.

Personal success and achieving personal goals is based upon how important you are to yourself. You are in charge of all this – it's your call. You can decide to go forward and make all these changes, or you can close the book now and just stop and say, 'Oh well, at least I gave it my best try,' and leave it at that. That probably would be your old behaviour, to get halfway or a third of the way through something and then not finish it. But we are talking about an ongoing process that does not finish.

If you are continually telling yourself that you are okay and that you are worth making changes for and worth striving for then, quite simply, your life can do nothing but get better. Yes, there'll be ups and downs and troubles will come your way, as they do to everybody. That doesn't mean you can't handle it in a more effective and productive way. We are not talking about sitting down and thinking about it – we are talking about getting up and doing it. The very fact that you've got this far in the book tells us that you are committed to achieving your goals.

Let's have a look at a couple of strategies to help you protect the changes you've made so far. It's very important to erase all the old messages and self-doubts that you've had in your mind, because if you think about it, you've continually told yourself that you can't do things. As I said earlier on, negatives breed negatives. Continuity breeds success.

Let me say that again: negatives breed negatives. Continuity breeds success!

It's so important to keep the positive pictures in your mind. Get a picture of what success would look like for you and consider it as a present to yourself, probably the best one you will ever give yourself. It's a present that will never lose its usefulness.

▨ Turn your life around

Josephine and I were talking recently about the early days in my recovery and how difficult it was for me to remain positive for very long. I had started drinking and taking drugs by the age of 11, and continued with a trail of destruction until I was 34. There weren't too many positive things that had happened in my life and even if they had come along I wouldn't have taken them anyway, because I was always remorseful and walking round with a big chip on my shoulder as if the world owed me a favour. My real problem was that I needed to take responsibility, and stop denying to myself that I had a serious problem with drugs and alcohol. It took me until I was 34 years old to face up to the problem.

Once I did face up to it, I thought recovery was going to be easy. Just stop drinking and taking drugs, and everything will fall into place. I soon got a big wake-up call because I realized that through my behaviour I had upset a lot of people. I had alienated a lot of people in my life. I had got totally in my own way, so I had to re-learn how to live. One of the most effective ways was learning to affirm myself. To tell myself that I had a right to pick up the pieces of my life and to do something with myself but, believe me, this was not easy because there was such a strong negative side of me that was saying, 'What's the point? You're 34 years old, nothing will ever happen now, it's too late. In six years you'll be 40.'

I decided to stop listening to that negative voice. I started listening to the positive things that people were saying to me. For the first time in my life I started to take advice from other people who could see the whole picture, instead of the blinkered view I'd had of my life. I had to make a 360-degree change in every aspect of my being.

It was suggested early on in my recovery that I set some targets for myself. Realistic targets, not unrealistic ones, because it's very easy to set our goals to high, which means we're setting ourselves up to fail. In a way, for someone like me – and perhaps you are like this, too – who is used to sabotaging himself, then that is exactly what will happen if the goals are too high. The first rule is – don't set unrealistic targets.

When I came out of the rehabilitation clinic, I went for an interview for a job, in a five-star hotel in Guernsey that had just opened. They had advertised for kitchen assistants, which was basically a kitchen porter, just washing dishes and cleaning floors. I was restarting my life, and that was the something I was fit for doing.

I went along for the interview and I can remember waiting to see the personnel officer and right up to the time I saw her I was telling myself, 'You will never get this job, they won't take you, they won't want a drunk, a drug addict. If they find out what you've been doing with your life, they won't even finish the interview.' To counteract that negativity I remembered what had been said in the clinic, which was, 'Just tell the truth, Beechy. If you tell the truth, the only way is up.'

I went into the interview and, sure enough, the lady said to me, 'What have you been doing with your life, you are 34 years old and you're now coming to be a kitchen assistant. Tell me a little about yourself.' I took a deep breath and my whole body temperature changed and I started to shake inside and my eyes filled up. I took a deep breath and I told her the truth, that I was trying to pick up the pieces of a life ruined by alcohol and drugs and I was trying to do something better with myself. Guess what? She gave me the job. I was there for about six months and I decided that I was going to enter a competition that they had within the hotels in Guernsey. I asked the chef if he'd let me do a tray of hors d'oeuvres. He laughed but he said, 'Okay, you can do that.' I had no previous experience in catering but I was always creative musically and I thought to myself, well, why not? Why shouldn't I give it a go? Why shouldn't I ask? In a way I was asserting my bill of rights that I was talking to you about earlier on in the book: you have the right to ask for something. You may not get it, but you have the right to ask. That's exactly what I did and I won a second prize.

From there I couldn't believe it when I was given a certificate, as I had never been given anything like that in my life before. That was a first. I then went to catering college for a year. I was the oldest person in the class. I was like the old man, but I persevered and I finished the course. I ended up in charge of the little brasserie kitchen in the hotel where I had initially started washing the floors and cleaning the dishes. I suddenly realized that if I started to apply myself and set myself some goals and worked hard towards them, it was possible to achieve things that I had never achieved in my life before. I stayed in that hotel for another year and then I was offered the chance to train as a therapist in the treatment centre that I had gone to for my own alcohol and drug abuse. From there my career has spanned 20 years and I have travelled the world speaking at different conferences. I have held workshops for training therapists and have worked with some of the best therapists in the world. It's all happened because I took responsibility. I decided that something different was going to happen in my life. If nothing else, I was going to give it my best shot and not let anything get in the way. Someone once said to me that no one says 'no' in a fantasy, and that's why we fantasize. I decided to live out my fantasy, just go for it and not take 'no' for an answer.

There were plenty of times I felt like giving up when times got hard because I came from a background with no academic qualifications. I left school when I was 14 and had not even done my Eleven Plus exam. I had absolutely nothing in terms of education – I could only just about read and write. I am not telling you this so that you can think, 'Well done, Beechy. Haven't you turned your life around?' I am telling you this because I know that if you apply yourself, make the right decisions, continually work on yourself and be realistic, then you can achieve your goals. Think about it – if it's happened for me, why shouldn't it happen for you? Why shouldn't you improve your life? Why shouldn't you achieve your goals? There's nothing getting in your way, only you.

In this chapter I'm saying that you have got to get out of the way of yourself and affirm that positive side of you that will keep the negative side quiet. Achieving your goals is going to be independence for you. It will give you a feeling that you haven't experienced before. Yes, you will have achieved things in your life before, but to have made a game plan to achieve new things might be a first for you. The independence you will feel when you achieve these goals will be quite overwhelming. One of the things you've got to watch out for is when the old behaviour and the old habits creep back in. You've got to nip them in the bud very quickly. Remember, old habits are in past times, not in this new time. You've got to ask yourself, 'What are you holding on to? Why do you go back to this old behaviour?' Is it because it feels safer? Is it a behaviour that you've always known? If that's the case, just have a look at what you get out of it. The answer to that question will be – the same old thing.

You're on your way now. You've been working very hard throughout this book. You can't go forward if you are still looking back. It's time to let go and affirm yourself for letting go.

Be your own cheering crowd

Chapter 10
Focusing and finishing

❏ Build self-belief

❏ Beat self-limiting beliefs

❏ You do have time!

By now you will have done your plans and should be busily working through the micro-goals that you have set for yourselves. Just remember to keep SMART at all times during this process and you will stay on track. Not only do those skills and strategies help you keep focused and structured, they are also very motivational, which is the key to focusing and finishing. You need to be combining the two elements at all times: the planning, which should be measured and specific, with the strategy of achieving your set micro-goals, targets, and time frames, which generate motivation. Motivation is the fuel that will drive you forwards, so remember always to be realistic – it is better to exceed what you set out to do with your micro-goals or targets than to end up constantly falling short. If you do that you will find that the tank of motivation will dry up very quickly and it will be difficult to replenish it.

▓ Staying focused through being motivated

Let's look at the motivational elements built into the planning stage one more time – but this time we are concerned with keeping you focused. Using micro-goals can build motivation and keep it going. As a result of being motivated it is easier to stay focused and you are propelled towards finishing and achieving your goal. We will all recognize how, if we start to feel that we are attempting the impossible, our focus goes and we just grind to a mental standstill. Instead of being able to conjure up images of achieving our goals and the incredible feeling that would bring, we probably all let that screen go blank and we are just left feeling that it's impossible. That then kicks off the negative tapes that we play in our heads: 'I can't do it.' 'This is impossible.' 'I should have known better.'

▓ Don't be afraid to ask for help

If you are learning a new skill or building on an existing skill, think about getting some tuition to give you the best possible start. There are lots of courses available at colleges and adult learning centres and they are often incredibly inexpensive, considering what they offer. If you are reluctant to seek the help of a teacher or trainer, ask yourself why. As we said earlier, some of you will have some quite negative messages about being taught – we have worked with many people who say that their school days left them feeling inadequate, if not stupid. Some have said that they are almost phobic about being in a 'learning situation' – they picture it as stressful and shaming. Why not consider giving yourself one more chance to have a positive experience? In fact, if you are considering signing up for a course, why not break the ice by speaking to a tutor or teacher about your fears?

Unfortunately, we often enlist the help of people who have knowledge of what we want to learn, but are not skilled teachers, and we wonder why we have a negative experience. If you really cannot afford to enlist the help of a teacher, or feel afraid to do so, think about the assets of a skilled teacher. You can, of course, use all the wonderful manuals and websites that exist, but we just want you to think for a moment about how a teacher would motivate you, as well as helping you over hurdles.

How micro-goals help

Let's look at the motivating and focusing aspect of micro-goals through these examples.

1 Dieting. We have shown several examples in the book of how you should break your weight-loss goal down to a weekly target of, say, 2–3 lb. The mistake that most people make is that they want a big weight loss, they want it fast and they want to see results. Micro-goals can help break this self-defeating pattern with a lot of dieters. You agree only to lose 2–3 lb per week and stop focusing on the 3 stones. Micro-goals help you focus on the here and now, rather than focusing upon something that is simply too far in the distance. There is a difference between a) getting excited about your goal and feeling those feelings, and b) working over a period of time and doing what you need to do to maintain the motivation. Picturing and imagining yourself achieving your goal gives you the kick-start – you then need to use the micro-goals to keep you going and stop you from losing interest.

2 Stopping smoking. Micro-goals assist with this as they bring your focus to the here and now and will help you with the psychological problem of facing giving up. Anyone feels somewhat negative and deprived if they are saying, 'Well, here is a habit that I have had for a long time and I have enjoyed it, even if it doesn't do me any good. I am now never going to do it again.' In fact, most experts on stopping smoking discourage such negative language and get people to think about the positive things they are doing. Most people giving up smoking would choose to concentrate on 'one day at a time', not be sitting saying, 'This is it – I'm never going to smoke again.' Micro-goals help us focus on today, which is particularly useful with dieting, when stopping smoking and can also be helpful if you have a problem with alcohol.

3 Learning a new skill. This could be computer literacy, assertiveness skills, a new language, an instrument or driving – the list is absolutely endless. There are many skills that require a lot of learning and practice – and this often puts people off. Some of you may not have had a good experience of learning when you were younger and you may be full of 'tapes' that say, 'I'd never learn that,' 'I'm too stupid,' 'I'd only make a fool of myself, it will take too long and I just don't have the time.' Listening to those negative tapes is a bad habit which, by reading this book, you are leaning to break. Keep up with that good work but, in the meantime, you also need to use your micro-goal skills to keep you motivated – if something is going to take a lot of learning then you have to find a way of 'fooling yourself' into accepting the time it will take, rather than being defeated by it:

Say, for example, your goal is learning to play a musical instrument – hundreds of people have shared with us that they would love to do that, but most people will also say, 'It's too hard,' 'It would take too long,' 'I can't read music – where would I start?' It has to be one of the most popular goals when it comes to learning something, and it is probably also one that people talk about but never achieve. What you have to understand from the outset is that there is a lot to learn and there is a lot of practising to do, but it doesn't make it impossible – it just makes it hard! But even so, it doesn't have to be 'hard work', particularly if you use micro-goals to help you break the task ahead down into smaller parts that you can master and then move on. People should also be careful of their expectations: you might have a friend who has played the piano since she was five years old. Don't keep comparing yourself with her. Concentrate on *your* achievements on the piano, instead of looking at someone who's been playing for 20 or 30 years.

Remember that contentment occurs when expectations meet with reality. In other words, keep your expectations reasonable and you will be pleasantly surprised. Approaching learning to play the piano using micro-goals will mean that you set a small goal for the week and focus on that – don't focus on the bigger picture, because then you feel as if you are standing at the bottom of a very high mountain and peering up at it. You feel defeated before you start. Micro-goals break everything down into manageable portions and you don't move on until you have achieved that micro-goal. The fact that you achieve your micro-goal will give you the motivation to tackle the next and the next and the one after that...

4 A goal associated with a life-change. Some goals can involve doing something that can impact very greatly on your life – they could possibly change your life, and therefore feel potentially risky. Setting micro-goals can keep you focused, but also help you 'feel' your way towards your goal and don't involve trying to take a big decision – instead, you can explore along the way and implement change if it feels right for you to do so. Changing your job is a good example. If you constantly flirt with the idea – do lots of talking but take no action, have a look at setting micro-goals to see if that will get you moving and keep you focused. Good micro-goals would include researching job options and attending interviews , which will help you make a considered and informed decision. You would, basically, edge your way towards the goal and then probably find that the balance naturally tips, so that the final push towards your goal doesn't feel like such a big step – it will simply feel right.

Micro-goals in action

Home decorating is another popular goal that often works well when broken down into micro-goals. If you do have several rooms that you want to decorate you will need to prioritize and only do one room at a time – it is a very good idea not to mess the whole house up. Try to keep some living spaces presentable so you can escape the decorating. The disruption that's sure to be involved as well as the time it takes to decorate properly can make a lot of people talk endlessly and do nothing!

Let's look at Jennifer:

Our whole house needs decorating. It is real mess and hasn't been touched for years. We bought it six months ago and of course we now don't have much spare cash. Luckily, structurally it is sound and all the window fames are okay – so it needs major cosmetic surgery. One big mistake is that we have tried to do a bit of a rush job on it and it just looks a mess. The house has a lounge/diner, kitchen, two bedrooms, bathroom and hall and stairs. It also has a tiny garden.

As we entertain a lot and enjoy cooking and watching DVDs we've decided to prioritize the lounge/diner and the kitchen. As the kitchen is too expensive to replace, we are going to have to just give it a face-lift. As we have a spare bedroom we are going to put the TV and the settee up there so we have a bolt hole. This will stop us from rushing because we are so fed up with the mess.

Our micro-goals and targets will be:

Move TV and settee upstairs into spare bedroom and make that look comfortable. Do this in the course of one evening and then stop.

Move rest of furniture into middle of lounge/diner and cover. Do this in the course of one evening and then stop.

I've set these time targets because we tend to go at jobs like lunatics – then we get exhausted and then it just all turns into an ordeal and we get fed up because we are tired. Then we start rushing and we just do a botched job.

Strip off existing wallpaper (*which we hate – we hate doing preparation*). We will do one hour each night and two hours a day at the weekend – there is quite a lot to do, so I don't think we'll get it all done during the week. We have set these time targets because we hate this part of the work but if we definitely commit to one hour during the evenings we are giving ourselves permission to stop when the hour's up – or if we feel okay we can do a bit more.

If we do this we are going to give ourselves a treat of going out when we have finished and having a Chinese meal – we love Chinese food and as money is short this will be a big incentive.

Fill in cracks. We'd spend one evening doing this because we don't mind filling.

Re-paper and paint, we'd save this for a weekend because we feel it could be difficult to stop and start but we quite enjoy this part so we'd be happy to spend the weekend.

Get new curtains and soft furnishings – this will also be a treat.

You can see how this couple use micro-goals and time settings to maintain their motivation and focus. They were very clear that some parts of decorating were just too boring, so they broke those tasks down in terms of time and also avoided getting themselves over-tired when they first started. They also haven't built themselves some sort of a mountain. They know what they don't like to do and, like most human beings, if we can avoid certain steps we will – which, again, is why people don't make their goals because they have missed out vital steps or rushed.

Jennifer and her partner know that the preparation is key to doing a job and they have committed to only doing one-hour stretches during the week. Obviously, if they felt like doing more they could. This type of strategy will work well for any goal. We also like the fact that they built some rewards into their plan, which is a nice motivational tool. Do think about what you can do to reward yourselves.

■ Building self-belief

Self-belief is not something we can teach you in a few paragraphs, but some of the exercises we have taken you through in this book will have started you on the road to believing more and more in yourself. Remember in terms of focusing and finishing that you have to work hard on believing you are going to achieve your goal. Some millionaires were recently asked for a television programme:

'Did you ever doubt that your plan would succeed?' Their answers were all exactly the same: a resounding 'no'.

As we have said many times, part of succeeding at anything – it might be a small goal, or it might be something much bigger and grander – you yourself have to believe that you can do it. You have to 'picture' yourself doing it and feel the feelings and behave like a winner. We can imagine the faces that some of you are pulling as you are reading this – but we are being serious. You have to stop holding yourselves back. You are capable of more than you will ever know – all you need to do is say 'I have the right to try ...'

The millionaires were also asked the question about whether they fear failure and again their responses were interesting. They didn't! They accepted that sometimes things didn't work out or went wrong but they used the experience as a positive one – they would amend their plans as a result or use the 'failure' as a positive tool to do something differently next time. Now you could say they have the luxury of thinking like that because they are millionaires and that would be a fair point, but we imagine that most of them thought like that long before they became successful financially.

■ Beating self-limiting beliefs

Earlier on we talked about self-limiting beliefs, which are also something that you can continue to work on long after you have finished reading this book. The sad thing is that we so often really don't know our true potential. This could be due to negative experiences at school, which may lead us to tell ourselves that we are stupid and incapable of learning. People feel scarred by these experiences and shy away from situations in which they might have to learn something because the association is that learning involves being shamed and embarrassed.

> Self-belief often means that you have to start by doing battle with self-limited beliefs. Here are some examples of self-limiting beliefs: 'I can't learn.' 'I'm no good at organizing.' 'People like me don't get on in business.' As one of our favourite sayings goes, 'the list is endless'. Remember that to be able to focus and finish you need to be your own crowd cheering you on to the finishing line. Imagine that scenario – what would they be saying if they really wanted you to cross the finishing line first?

▶ Go on – you can do it.
▶ Don't stop – you're almost there.
▶ Just keep going – you're going to win.
▶
▶ You need to start being your own 'crowd' cheering yourself on. Do it from
▶ now on.

■ You do have the time – don't lose focus

As we start to near our own finishing line, which is the end of this book, we wanted to take some time to talk about creating the time to make your goal work. Many of you will struggle to find the time to focus on yourself, your ideas and your goals and this, again, is why micro-goals can be an excellent solution to those of you who constantly battle against time.

If we wait until we have time, we probably will be retiring – and even then there might not be enough time. Some of you really will find there is no time to add anything else to your life. You might have young children, you could be studying and working, you might be working long hours, you might be nursing someone who is ill or you might have your own health problems and be spending a lot of time attending doctor's and hospital appointments. So, when you think about making time for your goal, you probably just see the impossibility of doing it.

If this is happening, or you are part-way through to achieving your goal and you start to feel you just don't have the time, stop and rethink the time frames you have set for yourself. No one has said that a goal has to be achieved in the fastest time possible. Remember that one of the SMART skills is about being realistic, so give yourself permission to take the time you need – if you can only steal small bits of time, so be it. If you are determined, you will do it.

We spoke a few paragraphs ago about becoming your own cheering crowd that calls out to you when you may be flagging or feeling that you don't have that last ounce of strength to continue on. Well, we'd like you to experience this very nice piece of imagery about finishing. It's a fun piece. It is exhilarating, but we are sure that it will get you nicely fired-up about just how good it can feel to finish what you have set out to do, and how wonderful it is to cross that finishing line a winner.

Read this next passage and then close your eyes and imagine it on the screen that we have asked you to use before:

Imagine that you are a world-class jockey, and we mean world class. You are a legend in your own time – you are unstoppable and your skills defy imagination. You are on the back of the fastest and safest horse in the world. Don't worry, you have all the skills to ride him – so don't be afraid. Nothing can go wrong and nothing will. So imagine yourself in that race. It is a gloriously sunny autumn day. The trees are copper as the sun shines through them; the course ahead is golden and inviting and magical. The gates have opened. You feel the surge of power from behind as the horse's hindquarters engage. You feel his hind legs striking the ground and pushing hard. You are out and galloping. You are surrounded by others trying to achieve the same goal, but you are going to win. You are so determined to win. You are saying to yourself, 'I can do it, I am going to do it, I'm a winner.' You aren't necessarily out at the front straight away, because you are a true tactician, but you are moving all the time. You are not just using the sheer speed of the horse, you are using your brain and that is what makes you the greatest. Just pause for a moment and feel the wind on your face – you are wearing racing goggles to protect your eyes and you have a skullcap on, but the wind still brushes against you as you race. You feel the air around your nose and mouth and you are aware of your heart thumping and the adrenalin flowing. You can hear the sound of the hooves hitting the ground – you can hear your breathing – you can hear the horse – you can hear the sound of the other horse – you can hear the crowd start to make a noise. They are cheering. They are shouting your name. They are yelling, 'Go on, you can do it!' Their shouts get louder and more rhythmical, like a chant. You move another place closer and then you are in the final furlong. The horse stretches out under you. You feel his hindquarters still powering from behind. You start to kick that bit harder. You are going to win. Nothing is going to stop you. You edge your way out in front and the horse seems to find another gear. He is romping home. You glance back – no one can catch you – you have another 100 yards to go and you can luxuriate in the feeling that you are going to make it – you are going to win and nothing will stop you. You heart beats faster and faster – you feel high – you cross the line –

you throw your hands in the air – you're burying your face in the horse's neck – he is sweating and breathing hard – you feel like you have just taken the most powerful drug in the world – the drug of success. You are a winner. You've done it ...

Put the book down and imagine that race. Imagine the fantastic feelings throughout the race but, most important of all, those feelings when the end is in sight and you know that you are going to do it. Project that image, project those feelings, those sensations, those thoughts on to your screen. See the rider, see the horse, see the race and then step into that image. Let that image be you. You are going to win that race. It doesn't matter how big or how small it is – you can achieve your goal and you, too, can feel like that champion jockey.

More essential guides available in the Personal Development series from
BBC Books:

*The Confidence Plan: Essential Steps
to A New You*
Sarah Litvinoff
Publication date: March 2004
ISBN: 0563 48763 1
CD ISBN: 0563 52336 0

*Starting Out: Essential Steps To Your
Dream Your Career*
Philippa Lamb and Nigel Cassidy
Publication date: August 2004
ISBN: 0563 52140 6
CD ISBN: 0563 52389 1

*Be Creative:Essential Steps to
Revitalise Your Work and Life*
Guy Claxton and Bill Lucas
Publication date: March 2004
ISBN: 0563 48764 X
CD ISBN: 0563 52331 X

*Negotiation: Essential Steps to Win
in Your Work & Life*
Hugh Wilbourn
Publication date: August 2004
ISBN: 0563 52148 1
CD ISBN: 0563 52394 8

*Find the Balance:Essential Steps to
Fulfilment in Your Work and Life*
Deborah Tom
Publication date: March 2004
ISBN: 0563 52138 4
CD ISBN: 0563 52341 7

*Embracing Change: Essential Steps
to Make Your Future Today*
Tony Buzan
Publication date: January 2005
ISBN: 0563 48762 3

All titles are available at good bookstores and online through the BBC shop at
www.bbcshop.com